Twentieth Century Poetry

HOUGHTON BO   LITERATURE

HOUGHTON
BOOKS IN
LITERATURE

ADVISORY EDITOR
KENNETH S. LYNN

Twentieth Century

Poetry

CAROL MARSHALL

HOUGHTON MIFFLIN COMPANY • BOSTON

NEW YORK   ATLANTA   GENEVA, ILLINOIS   DALLAS   PALO ALTO

ABOUT THE AUTHOR AND EDITOR

Carol Marshall has taught many subjects, from arithmetic to aesthetics, to many ages. She writes for the professional journals about literature — especially poetry — and art, and about the art of teaching. She is now teaching English at the Katherine Delmar Burke School in San Francisco.

Kenneth S. Lynn, advisory editor for the Houghton Books in Literature, is an authority in American literature. The author of *Mark Twain and Southwestern Humor* and *The Dream of Success: A Study of the Modern American Imagination,* he is also preeminent for his editing of classic American writers. Dr. Lynn is now a professor at the Johns Hopkins University.

Printed in the U. S. A.

Hardcover Edition ISBN: 0-395-12358-5

Softcover Edition ISBN: 0-395-12357-7

Library of Congress Catalogue Card Number: 74-146186

ACKNOWLEDGMENTS

The editor wishes to thank the following publishers and authors or their representatives for permission to use copyrighted materials:

Atheneum Publishers, Inc., for "Lemuel's Blessing" from *The Moving Target* by W. S. Merwin, copyright © 1962 by W. S. Merwin. Originally appeared in *The New Yorker;* for "The Removal" from *The Carrier of Ladders* by W. S. Merwin, copyright © 1970. Appeared originally in *Harper's Bazaar.*

City Lights Books, for "A Supermarket in California" and "Wild Orphan," copyright © 1956, 1959 by Allen Ginsberg.

Continental Total Media Project, Inc., for "Suzanne" by Leonard Cohen, © 1966 by Project Seven Music, a div. of C.T.M.P., Inc., New York.

Corinth Books, for "Preface to a Twenty Volume Suicide Note," copyright © 1961 by LeRoi Jones; for "John Muir on Mt. Ritter," copyright © 1960 by Gary Snyder.

Owen Dodson, for his poem "Yardbird's Skull."

Doubleday & Company, Inc., for "On Giving a Son to the Sea," copyright © 1969 by James Dickey, from *The Eyebeaters, Blood, Victory, Madness, Buckhead and Mercy* by James Dickey; for "Dolor," "Elegy for Jane," "The Waking," and "I Knew a Woman" by Theodore Roethke. "Dolor," copyright 1943 by the Modern Poetry Association; "Elegy for Jane," copyright 1950 by Theodore Roethke; "The Waking," copyright 1948 by Theodore Roethke; "I Knew a Woman," copyright 1954 by Theodore Roethke; all from the book *The Collected Poems of Theodore Roethke.*

Farrar, Straus & Giroux, Inc., for "A Camp in the Prussian Forest" from *Complete Poems* by Randall Jarrell, copyright © 1955 by Randall Jarrell; for "Skunk Hour" from *Life Studies* by Robert Lowell, copyright © 1958 by Robert Lowell.

Harcourt Brace Jovanovich, Inc., for "The Hollow Men," "Marina," and "Journey of the Magi" from *Collected Poems 1909–1962* by T. S. Eliot, copyright 1936 by Harcourt Brace Jovanovich, Inc., copyright © 1963, 1964 by T. S. Eliot; for "Quaker Hero, Burning" and "June," copyright © 1966 by Bink Noll, reprinted from his volume, *The Feast;* for "Love Calls Us to the Things of This World" from *Things of This World,* © 1956 by Richard Wilbur; for "if everything happens that can't be done," copyright 1944 by E. E. Cummings, reprinted from his volume *Poems 1923–1954;* for "Stumpfoot" and "Things" from *Selected Poems,* © 1965 by Louis Simpson; for "My Great-Grandfather's Slaves," copyright © 1965 by Wendell Berry, reprinted from his volume *Openings.*

Harper & Row, Publishers, Inc. for "Hearing Men Shout at Night on Macdougal Street" from *The Light Around the Body* by Robert Bly, copyright © 1959 by Robert Bly; for "The Dump" copyright © 1969 by The New Yorker Magazine Inc., from *The Alligator Bride: Poems New and Selected* by Donald Hall, copyright © 1969 by Donald Hall; for "The Arrival of the Bee Box" from *Ariel* by Sylvia Plath, copyright © 1963 by Ted Hughes; for "We Real Cool" from *Selected Poems* by Gwendolyn Brooks, copyright © 1959 by Gwendolyn Brooks; for "The Concealment: Ishi, the Last Wild Indian" from *The Rescued Year* by William Stafford, copyright © 1965 by William E. Stafford; for "MONET: Les Nymphéas" from *After Experience* by W. D. Snodgrass, copyright © 1963 by W. D. Snodgrass.

Holt, Rinehart and Winston, Inc., for "Spring Pools" from *The Poetry of Robert Frost,* edited by Edward Connery Lathem, copyright 1916, 1928 by Holt, Rinehart and Winston, Inc., copyright 1944, © 1956 by Robert Frost.

Katherine Hoskins, for her poems "When Snow Falls" and "The Youngest Schizophrene."

LeRoi Jones and the Ronald Hobbs Literary Agency, for "Lines to García Lorca " by LeRoi Jones, copyright © 1964 by LeRoi Jones. Reprinted from *New Negro Poets: U.S.A.,* edited by Langston Hughes.

Alfred A. Knopf, Inc., for "Junior Addict," copyright © 1963 by Langston Hughes, reprinted from *The Panther and the Lash* by Langston Hughes; for "Peter Quince at the Clavier," copyright 1923 and renewed 1951 by Wallace Stevens, reprinted from *The Collected Poems of Wallace Stevens;* for "Leviathan" from *Green with Beasts* by W. S. Merwin, published 1956 by Alfred A. Knopf, Inc.

The Macmillan Company, for "The Second Coming," "The Wild Swans at Coole," "Father and Child," "A Deep-Sworn Vow," and "Leda and the Swan" from *Collected Poems* by William Butler Yeats. "The Second Coming," copyright 1924 by The Macmillan Company, renewed 1952 by Bertha Georgie Yeats. "The Wild Swans at Coole," copyright 1919 by The Macmillan Company, renewed 1947 by Bertha Georgie Yeats. "Father and Child," copyright 1933 by The Macmillan Company, renewed 1961 by Bertha Georgie Yeats. "A Deep-Sworn Vow," copyright 1919 by The Macmillan Company, renewed 1947 by Bertha Georgie Yeats. "Leda and the Swan," copyright 1928 by The Macmillan Company, renewed 1961 by Bertha Georgie Yeats.

William Morrow and Company, Inc., for "Love Poem" from *The Iron Pastoral* by John Frederick Nims. Published by William Sloane Associates, Inc. Copyright 1947 by John Frederick Nims.

The Nation, for "The Third World" by Lawrence Ferlinghetti.

New Directions Publishing Corporation, for "The Raid" from *The Residual Years* by William Everson, copyright 1948 by New Directions Publishing Corporation; for "Don't let that horse" and "Christ Climbed Down" from *A Coney Island of the Mind* by Lawrence Ferlinghetti, copyright © 1958 by Lawrence Ferlinghetti; for "There died a myriad" from "Hugh Selwyn Mauberley" and "Exile's Letter" from *Personae* by Ezra Pound, copyright 1926 by Ezra Pound; for "The Gift" from *Pictures from Brueghel,* copyright © 1962 by William Carlos Williams; for "What Were They Like?" from *The Sorrow Dance* by Denise Levertov, copyright 1966 by Denise Levertov Goodman; for "The Breathing" from *O Taste and See* by Denise Levertov, copyright © 1963 by Steuben Glass, first published in "Poetry in Crystal"; for "Somnambulistic Ballad," translated by Roy and Mary Campbell; by permission of New Directions Publishing Corporation, agents for the estate of Federico García Lorca, publishers of the *Selected Poems* of Federico García Lorca, copyright 1955 by New Directions Publishing Corporation, all rights reserved; for "Fern Hill," "Do Not Go Gentle into That Good Night," and "The Hunchback in the Park" from *Collected Poems* by Dylan Thomas, copyright 1943, 1946 by New Directions Publishing Corporation, copyright 1952 by Dylan Thomas; for "These," "Tract," "Complaint," "The Trees," and "Spring and All" from *Collected Poems* by William Carlos Williams, copyright 1938 by William Carlos Williams.

Harold Ober Associates, Inc., for "Fog-Horn" and "Grandfather in the Old Men's Home" from *The Drunk in the Furnace* by W. S. Merwin, copyright © 1957 by W. S. Merwin.

Orenstein, Arrow & Silverman, for "The 59th Street Bridge Song" © Paul Simon. Used with permission of Charing Cross Music, Inc.

Oxford University Press, for "The Horses" from *Collected Poems* by Edwin Muir, copyright © 1960 by Willa Muir; for "The Fury of Aerial Bombardment"; from *Collected Poems 1930–1960* by Richard Eberhart, copyright © 1960 by Richard Eberhart.

Random House, Inc., for "The Child Next Door" from "To a Little Girl, One Year Old, in a Ruined Fortress," copyright © 1955 by Robert Penn Warren, reprinted from *Promises: Poems 1954–1956* by Robert Penn Warren; for "Sext" from "Horae Canonicae," copyright © 1955 by W. H. Auden, reprinted from *Collected Shorter Poems 1927–1957* by W. H. Auden; for "In Memory of W. B. Yeats" and "Musée des Beaux Arts," copyright 1940, renewed 1968 by W. H. Auden, reprinted from *Collected Shorter Poems 1927–1957* by W. H. Auden; for "Signpost," copyright 1935 and renewed 1963 by Donnan Jeffers and Garth Jeffers, reprinted from *The Selected Poetry of Robinson Jeffers;* for "Continent's End," copyright 1924 and renewed 1952 by Robinson Jeffers, reprinted from *The Selected Poetry of Robinson Jeffers;* for "Drug Store," copyright 1941 and renewed 1969 by Karl Shapiro, reprinted from *Selected Poems* by Karl Shapiro; for "When suffering is everywhere," copyright © 1964 by Karl Shapiro, reprinted from *Selected Poems* by Karl Shapiro; for "In the second-best hotel in Tokyo," copyright © 1963 by Karl Shapiro, reprinted from *Selected Poems* by Karl Shapiro; for "Skiers" from "In the Mountains," copyright © 1967 by Robert Penn Warren, reprinted from *Incarnations: Poems 1966–1968* by Robert Penn Warren.

Charles Scribner's Sons, for "Evolution," copyright 1954 by May Swenson, from *To Mix with Time* by May Swenson; for "The Lowering (Arlington Cemetery, June 8, 1968)," copyright © 1969 May Swenson, from *Iconographs* by May Swenson. First appeared in *The New Yorker;* for "Song" from *Words* by

Robert Creeley, copyright © 1962, 1963, 1964, 1967 Robert Creeley; for "The Name" and "I Know a Man," from *For Love* by Robert Creeley, copyright © 1962 Robert Creeley.

Steuben Glass, for "Birds and Fishes," copyright 1963 Steuben Glass.

The Viking Press, Inc., for "Summer Night" and "For Anne" from *Selected Poems: 1956–1968* by Leonard Cohen, copyright in all countries of the International Copyright Union, all rights reserved; for "Bavarian Gentians" from *The Complete Poems of D. H. Lawrence, Volume II,* edited by Vivian de Sola Pinto and F. Warren Roberts, copyright 1933 by Frieda Lawrence, all rights reserved.

Wesleyan University Press, for "As I Step Over a Puddle at the End of Winter, I Think of an Ancient Chinese Governor" from *The Branch Will Not Break* by James Wright, copyright © 1961, 1962 by James Wright; for "The Heaven of Animals" and "Deer Among Cattle" from *Poems 1957–1967* by James Dickey, copyright © 1961, 1965 by James Dickey. "The Heaven of Animals" was first published in *The New Yorker;* for "Bus Stop" from *Night Light* by Donald Justice, copyright © 1966 by Donald Justice; for "Brooding" and "For One Moment" from *Figures of the Human* by David Ignatow, copyright © 1948, 1962 by David Ignatow; for "Miners" from *The Branch Will Not Break* by James Wright, copyright © 1961 by James Wright. This poem was first published in *Poetry;* for "Saint Judas" from *Saint Judas* by James Wright.

CONTENTS

The Things of This World

Love

My Townspeople

The Box Is Locked

Twentieth Century Poetry

Introductory

Poetry is many things in the twentieth century that it has never quite been before.

In a time of continuing and catastrophic change, poets have changed the tune of poetry, changed its shape — changed its very nerve of feeling in order to record a new and often numbing reality.

Poetry has also had to fight merely to survive the cataract of words which engulfs us daily: news, magazines, songs, advertisements, directives, information, books, books, books. Most of these abuse words: they manipulate them, blur the edges of meaning, wear words out. Yet poetry has had to use these same words — in the service of the most precise meaning, the subtlest communication. For, as Mallarmé the French poet observed, "Poems are made of words, not ideas."

Modern poets are constantly refurbishing words: freshening them by new juxtapositions, new contexts, new rhythms. Poets have also stayed with the common words of our language — largely kept away from esoteric speech, and decorative effects, and everything that used to be called "poetic diction."

Thus, when Robert Creeley at one extreme writes

> *What do you*
> *want, love. To be*
> *loved. What,*

he forces us to be freshly aware of the word itself, taken separately, stripped — and then of each word as part of the cluster, moving circularly, and creating different meanings as part of the sentence and of the stanza.

Dylan Thomas surely stands at the opposite extreme in his style — creating with matchless brilliance great rich swirls of design:

> *And nothing I cared, at my sky blue trades, that time allows*
> *In all his tuneful turning so few and such morning songs*
> *Before the children green and golden*
> *Follow him out of grace . . .*

New rhythms too match the changing pace of the twentieth century: its informality, its discords and spasms, its nostalgias. Old forms are wrenched and twisted by the terrible burden they bear:

> *I walk beside the prisoners to the road.*
> *Load on puffed load,*
> *Their corpses, stacked like sodden wood,*
> *Lie barred or galled with blood*
>
> *By the charred warehouse.*

— or they seem to mock a life that is empty and meaningless, though it clings to the old ways:

> *Lights are burning*
> *In quiet rooms*
> *Where lives go on*
> *Resembling ours.*

But traditional forms can still provide a strong expression for timeless themes that link us with all men who have stood and wondered:

> *The trees are in their autumn beauty,*
> *The woodland paths are dry,*
> *Under the October twilight the water*
> *Mirrors a still sky;*
> *Upon the brimming water among the stones*
> *Are nine-and-fifty swans.*

Largely, however, the twentieth century has seen wide experimentation with new forms. Poets make up their own rules, so that form is both created for a particular theme and also helps to shape it: custom-made. Symmetry and regularity are less obvious: a more organic growth has taken their place, often revealing complex and subtle inner textures. Here, in Theodore Roethke's "Elegy for Jane," the sound patterns rise and fall like the irregular rhythm of wind through trees:

> *I remember the neckcurls, limp and damp as tendrils;*
> *And her quick look, a sidelong pickerel smile;*

> *And how, once startled into talk, the light syllables*
> *leaped for her,*
> *And she balanced in the delight of her thought,*
> *A wren, happy, tail into the wind,*
> *Her song trembling the twigs and small branches.*

The poetry of this century manages to be at once personal, spare, and tough — "close to the bone," as Ezra Pound hoped for it. It is serious poetry: it speaks of the battlefields and fire storms of war, and its rotting aftermath — of the marketplace and the political scene, as well as of the rooms and gardens of our private lives. Often it has seemed very literally prophetic, as when W. B. Yeats wrote about the political disintegration and rule by terror between the two wars:

> *Things fall apart; the centre cannot hold;*
> *Mere anarchy is loosed upon the world,*
> *The blood-dimmed tide is loosed, and everywhere*
> *The ceremony of innocence is drowned;*
> *The best lack all conviction, while the worst*
> *Are full of passionate intensity.*

The poet has in a sense become the conscience of mankind. He has borne witness to the enormities of the twentieth century, and of the crass culture that has travestied its dearest traditions:

> *Christ climbed down*
> *from His bare Tree*
> *this year*
> *and ran away to where*
> *there were no gilded Christmas trees*
> *and no tinsel Christmas trees*
> *and no tinfoil Christmas trees*
> *and no pink plastic Christmas trees*
> *and no gold Christmas trees*
> *and no black Christmas trees*
> *and no . . .*

The poet may speak in mocking irony, as here; he may speak stridently, or with anger, love, sadness, tenderness. His voice is heard in many new places — in the streets or at rock concerts, for example — for there are no longer special times and places for poetry. Nor special subjects: the storehouse of taboos has been ransacked; whatever is of importance to the poet has become part of his poetry. Thus twentieth-century interest in psychology is reflected in the inward direction of much poetry. The phantasmagoria of the unconscious is the source of image making, as it always has been, but the dramatic action of the poem is more often within man's mind than in his public life. At the same time, bewildering changes in values and ways of living have forced the poet more and more to speak to us of his own personal experience, which is really the only thing that a person can be sure of. Yet, by his universal images and by the intensity of his feeling, he overcomes separation and shows us what it is to be a human being in the twentieth century. And we discover that his are also our own greatest concerns: we cannot help but respond, and enter into dialogue with him.

> *we're anything brighter than even the sun*
> *(we're everything greater*
> *than books*
> *might mean)*
> *we're everyanything more than believe*
> *(with a spin*
> *leap*
> *alive we're alive)*
> *we're wonderful one times one*

1

An Age of Anxiety

What crucial experiences have twentieth-century poets taken as subjects for their poetry? In the twentieth century man's superb scientific achievements have begun to outrun his control; wars have been continuous and devastating; part of the world lives in unprecedented opulence, the rest in poverty. The increasing mechanization and specialization of man's work have had the effect of fragmenting people's lives. The family unit has been threatened, traditional institutions questioned, and the importance of the individual diminished. With his old faiths crumbling, twentieth-century man finds himself alone, increasingly a stranger to himself and to his planet earth . . . The poet W. H. Auden has called this the "age of anxiety."

These themes of violence and alienation occur again and again in the poetry of the century. Poets see beneath the surface glitter of civilization to the impoverishment of spirit within. In their poetry they speak for human values, for a more humanly oriented world, worthy of man's best self. The poetic process itself keeps faith with man's unceasing creativity.

How do poets communicate their urgent sense of things gone wrong? What kinds of poems can speak to people numbed by shock? It is hard to find images strong enough; language strains to make itself heard; form tends to break down under such pressure. Sometimes a poem will seem to hold together only by the force of the passion it expresses. Order, memory, reason, love: the things that formerly united men are reflected in this poetry as in fragments of a broken mirror.

Most people in the Western world live in cities. Poets like Walt Whitman and Carl Sandburg used to write about them affectionately as gathering places of common enterprise. Here was the excitement of participation in the greater world, and the warmth of congenial companies of friends. But the cities have changed. Today the poets of the city write about the deadening routines of commerce, the anonymity of lives reduced to numbers, the irony of loneliness in the midst of crowds.

Dolor

Theodore Roethke

I have known the inexorable sadness of pencils,
Neat in their boxes, dolor of pad and paper-weight,
All the misery of manilla folders and mucilage,
Desolation in immaculate public places,
Lonely reception room, lavatory, switchboard,   5
The unalterable pathos of basin and pitcher,
Ritual of multigraph, paper-clip, comma,
Endless duplication of lives and objects.
And I have seen dust from the walls of institutions,
Finer than flour, alive, more dangerous than silica,   10
Sift, almost invisible, through long afternoons of tedium,
Dropping a fine film on nails and delicate eyebrows,
Glazing the pale hair, the duplicate grey standard faces.

Drug Store

Karl Shapiro

I do remember an apothecary,
*And hereabouts 'a dwells**

It baffles the foreigner like an idiom,
And he is right to adopt it as a form
Less serious than the living-room or bar;
    For it disestablishes the café,
Is a collective, and on basic country.   5

Not that it praises hygiene and corrupts
The ice-cream parlor and the tobacconist's

* from Shakespeare's Romeo and Juliet, 5.2.37–38.

Is it a center; but that the attractive symbols
     Watch over puberty and leer
Like rubber bottles waiting for sick-use.   10

Youth comes to jingle nickels and crack wise;
The baseball scores are his, the magazines
Devoted to lust, the jazz, the Coca-Cola,
     The lending-library of love's latest.
He is the customer; he is heroized.   15

And every nook and cranny of the flesh
Is spoken to by packages with wiles.
"Buy me, buy me," they whimper and cajole;
     The hectic range of lipsticks pouts,
Revealing the wicked and the simple mouth.   20

With scarcely any evasion in their eye
They smoke, undress their girls, exact a stance;
But only for a moment. The clock goes round;
     Crude fellowships are made and lost;
They slump in booths like rags, not even drunk.   25

1. These two poems hardly mention people: what do they nevertheless tell us about people's lives?

2. What is the tone of each poem — the attitude of the speaker
   toward his subject? What is your own response?

3. The quotation heading, from Shakespeare's *Romeo and Juliet*,
   implies a comparison with modern life. How does this comparison
   suggest the intention of the poem?

Bus Stop

Donald Justice

Lights are burning
In quiet rooms
Where lives go on
Resembling ours.

The quiet lives   5
That follow us —
These lives we lead
But do not own —

Stand in the rain
So quietly   10
When we are gone,
So quietly . . .

And the last bus
Comes letting dark
Umbrellas out: 15
Black flowers, black flowers.

And lives go on.
And lives go on
Like sudden lights
At street corners   20

Or like the lights
In quiet rooms
Left on for hours,
Burning, burning.

The Dump

Donald Hall

The trolley has stopped long since.
There is no motorman.
The passenger thinks
he is at the end of the line.
No, it is past the end. Around him   5
is the graveyard of trolleys,
thousands of oblongs tilted
at angles to each other,
yellow paint chipped.
Stepping outside, he sees smoke rising   10
from holes in roofs.
Old men live here, in narrow houses full of rugs,
in this last place.

1. What states of mind do these last two poems create? Have you had experiences that help you to understand these poems? Explain in what way.

2. Don't be misled by the apparent casualness of "The Dump." In what way can it be seen as a parable of modern life?

3. Does the dreamlike quality of these two poems weaken their social urgency, or strengthen it?

4. Can you explain how the simple language of "Bus Stop" generates intense feeling and meaning? How does the form of the poem strengthen the meaning?

The next poems were written by three of the most influential poets of the century and have all played a large part in the development of later poetry. Each of these poets describes, in prophetic images, the disintegration and despair overtaking society. Yeats's poem was written in 1919, Eliot's in 1925, and Williams's in 1938.

The Second Coming

William Butler Yeats

Turning and turning in the widening gyre*
The falcon cannot hear the falconer;
Things fall apart; the centre cannot hold;
Mere anarchy is loosed upon the world,
The blood-dimmed tide is loosed, and everywhere   5
The ceremony of innocence is drowned;
The best lack all conviction, while the worst
Are full of passionate intensity.

Surely some revelation is at hand;
Surely the Second Coming is at hand.   10
The Second Coming! Hardly are those words out
When a vast image out of *Spiritus Mundi**
Troubles my sight: somewhere in sands of the desert
A shape with lion body and the head of a man,
A gaze blank and pitiless as the sun,   15
Is moving its slow thighs, while all about it
Reel shadows of the indignant desert birds.
The darkness drops again; but now I know
That twenty centuries of stony sleep
Were vexed to nightmare by a rocking cradle,   20
And what rough beast, its hour come round at last,
Slouches towards Bethlehem to be born?

1. gyre: *the bird's spiraling flight.*
12. *Spiritus Mundi: in Yeats's mystical system, the world's collective memory from which man draws images. Literally, spirit of the world.*

1.   The horrors of World War I led Yeats to believe that the end of the
     Christian era was approaching. Looking back at "The Second
     Coming" in 1936 when totalitarian governments were on the rise,
     Yeats wrote in a letter that the poem had "foretold what is happen-
     ing. I am not callous, every nerve trembles with horror at what is

happening in Europe, 'the ceremony of innocence is drowned.'"
How does this enlarge the meaning of the poem? Has subsequent
history further confirmed Yeats's premonition?

2. How has Yeats transformed the familiar symbolism of myth and
   religious tradition — for instance that of the Second Coming of
   Christ? with what effect? Where do human values or human beings
   fit into this prophetic vision?

3. Read the poem aloud. How do the abrupt stops, the staggered
   sentences, and the rhythm breaks help to intensify the meaning of
   the poem?

The Hollow Men

T. S. Eliot

Mistah Kurtz* — he dead.
                            A penny for the Old Guy†

I

We are the hollow men
We are the stuffed men
Leaning together
Headpiece filled with straw. Alas!
Our dried voices, when   5
We whisper together
Are quiet and meaningless
As wind in dry grass
Or rats' feet over broken glass
In our dry cellar   10

Shape without form, shade without colour,
Paralysed force, gesture without motion;

* Mistah Kurtz: *"a lost violent soul"* in *Joseph Conrad's* Heart of Darkness.
† A penny . . . Guy: *slogan of English children begging pennies for fire-
works on Guy Fawkes Day. The day commemorates Fawkes's unsuccess-
ful attempt to blow up the Houses of Parliament. Kurtz and Fawkes, men
of action, are contrasted to "hollow" modern men.*

Those who have crossed
With direct eyes,* to death's other Kingdom*
Remember us — if at all — not as lost   15
Violent souls, but only
As the hollow men
The stuffed men.

                II
Eyes I dare not meet in dreams
In death's dream kingdom   20
These do not appear:
There, the eyes are
Sunlight on a broken column
There, is a tree swinging
And voices are   25
In the wind's singing
More distant and more solemn
Than a fading star.

Let me be no nearer
In death's dream kingdom   30
Let me also wear
Such deliberate disguises
Rat's coat, crowskin, crossed staves
In a field
Behaving as the wind behaves   35
No nearer —

Not that final meeting
In the twilight kingdom

14. direct eyes: *These belong to those whose lives were committed to something positive, whether good or evil.* death's other Kingdom: *the kingdom of those who are actually physically dead (as opposed to the living death of the hollow men).*

III

This is the dead land
This is cactus land   40
Here the stone images
Are raised, here they receive
The supplication of a dead man's hand
Under the twinkle of a fading star.

Is it like this   45
In death's other kingdom
Waking alone
At the hour when we are
Trembling with tenderness
Lips that would kiss   50
Form prayers to broken stone.

IV

The eyes are not here
There are no eyes here
In this valley of dying stars
In this hollow valley   55
This broken jaw of our lost kingdoms

In this last of meeting places
We grope together
And avoid speech
Gathered on this beach of the tumid river   60

Sightless, unless
The eyes reappear
As the perpetual star
Multifoliate rose*
Of death's twilight kingdom   65
The hope only
Of empty men.

64. rose: *Christ's emblem, and Mary's.*

V

Here we go round the prickly pear
Prickly pear prickly pear
Here we go round the prickly pear   70
At five o'clock in the morning.

Between the idea
And the reality
Between the motion
And the act   75
Falls the Shadow
                    For Thine is the Kingdom

Between the conception
And the creation
Between the emotion   80
And the response
Falls the Shadow
                              Life is very long

Between the desire
And the spasm   85
Between the potency
And the existence
Between the essence
And the descent
Falls the Shadow   90
                    For Thine is the Kingdom

For Thine is
Life is
For Thine is the

This is the way the world ends   95
This is the way the world ends
This is the way the world ends
Not with a bang but a whimper.

1. Study the form of the last poem, the arrangement of words on the page: notice the broken lines, the variety of rhythms which interrupt each other, the fragmented syntax, the disruptions of thought. How do these things affect the experience of reading the poem?

2. Describe the voice and the tone of the speaker. How prevalent is the tone of irony? What is the relevance of the allusions to ritual and to games? of the antiphonal pattern (alternating responses)?

3. How do all these elements mentioned help to define the twentieth-century consciousness as Eliot saw it?

These

William Carlos Williams

are the desolate, dark weeks
when nature in its barrenness
equals the stupidity of man.

The year plunges into night
and the heart plunges   5
lower than night

to an empty, windswept place
without sun, stars or moon
but a peculiar light as of thought

that spins a dark fire —   10
whirling upon itself until,
in the cold, it kindles

to make a man aware of nothing
that he knows, not loneliness
itself — Not a ghost but   15

would be embraced — emptiness,
despair — (They
whine and whistle) among

the flashes and booms of war;
houses of whose rooms   20
the cold is greater than can be thought,

the people gone that we loved,
the beds lying empty, the couches
damp, the chairs unused —

Hide it away somewhere   25
out of the mind, let it get roots
and grow, unrelated to jealous

ears and eyes — for itself.
In this mine they come to dig — all.
Is this the counterfoil to sweetest   30

music? The source of poetry that
seeing the clock stopped, says,
The clock has stopped

that ticked yesterday so well?
and hears the sound of lakewater   35
splashing — that is now stone.

1. "It isn't what [the poet] *says* that counts as a work of art," William
    Carlos Williams once wrote, "it's what he makes, with such in-
    tensity of perception that it lives with an intrinsic movement of its
    own to verify its authenticity." Comment on "These" in the light
    of Williams's own statement about the nature of a poem.
2. Compare "These" with "The Hollow Men" and "The Second
    Coming." Which contains the most highly charged images, in
    your opinion? Which poem do you feel is most relevant to the
    present?

Robinson Jeffers, a contemporary of Williams and Eliot, suggested in "Signpost" a way to get "out of the pit" — by rediscovering God, through the things of his creation. But the poems of W. S. Merwin, Karl Shapiro, and Lawrence Ferlinghetti which follow suggest that contemporary man has lost touch with anything transcendent.

In reading the next few poems, try a way that the poet May Swenson suggests: "Something can be felt about [the poem] before beginning to read: its profile on the page, its regular or irregular pattern of stanzas, length of line, their symmetry, its wide or thin shape, its look of bulk or lightness. . . . I suppress attention to the content, and quickly read through the poem for its sound alone. I want to determine the mainsprings of its music before releasing its images into consciousness."

Signpost

Robinson Jeffers

Civilized, crying how to be human again: this will tell
    you how.
Turn outward, love things, not men, turn right away
    from humanity,
Let that doll lie. Consider if you like how the lilies
    grow,
Lean on the silent rock until you feel its divinity
Make your veins cold, look at the silent stars, let your
    eyes   5
Climb the great ladder out of the pit of yourself and
    man.
Things are so beautiful, your love will follow your
    eyes;
Things are the God, you will love God, and not in
    vain,
For what we love, we grow to it, we share its nature.

At length
You will look back along the stars' rays and see that
    even   10
The poor doll humanity has a place under heaven.
Its qualities repair their mosaic around you, the chips
    of strength
And sickness; but now you are free, even to become
    human,
But born of the rock and the air, not of a woman.

Fog-Horn

W. S. Merwin

Surely that moan is not the thing
That men thought they were making, when they
Put it there, for their own necessities.
That throat does not call to anything human
But to something men had forgotten,   5
That stirs under fog. Who wounded that beast
Incurably, or from whose pasture
Was it lost, full grown, and time closed round it
With no way back? Who tethered its tongue
So that its voice could never come   10
To speak out in the light of clear day,
But only when the shifting blindness
Descends and is acknowledged among us,
As though from under a floor it is heard,
Or as though from behind a wall, always   15
Nearer than we had remembered? If it
Was we that gave tongue to this cry
What does it bespeak in us, repeating
And repeating, insisting on something
That we never meant? We only put it there   20

To give warning of something we dare not
Ignore, lest we should come upon it
Too suddenly, recognize it too late,
As our cries were swallowed up and all hands lost.

When suffering is everywhere, that is of the nature of belief

Karl Shapiro

When suffering is everywhere, that is of the nature of
    belief. When the leaders are corrupted, Pope or
    Commissar, nor do the people flicker an eyelash,
    that is of the nature of belief. When there are
    anniversaries of battle or martyrdom, that is of   5
    the nature of belief. When there is the slogan
    Credo quia absurdum* or intellectual proof of
    the existence of God, that is of the nature of
    belief. When priests pray for victory and gen-
    erals invoke heaven, when prisons fill with   10
    children, that is of the nature of belief. When
    the word *evil* appears in newspapers, *moral* in
    the mouths of policemen, *culture* in the pre-
    pared speeches of politicians, all that is of the
    nature of belief. Belief makes blood flow. Belief   15
    infects the dead with more belief. Now it flows
    in our veins. Now it floats in the clouds.

7. Credo quia absurdum: "*I believe because it is absurd.*"

Christ Climbed Down

Lawrence Ferlinghetti

Christ climbed down
from His bare Tree
this year
and ran away to where
there were no rootless Christmas trees   5
hung with candycanes and breakable stars

Christ climbed down
from His bare Tree
this year
and ran away to where   10
there were no gilded Christmas trees
and no tinsel Christmas trees
and no tinfoil Christmas trees
and no pink plastic Christmas trees
and no gold Christmas trees   15
and no black Christmas trees
and no powderblue Christmas trees
hung with electric candles
and encircled by tin electric trains
and clever cornball relatives   20

Christ climbed down
from His bare Tree
this year
and ran away to where
no intrepid Bible salesmen   25
covered the territory
in two-tone cadillacs
and where no Sears Roebuck creches
complete with plastic babe in manger
arrived by parcel post   30

the babe by special delivery
and where no televised Wise Men
praised the Lord Calvert Whiskey

Christ climbed down
from His bare Tree   35
this year
and ran away to where
no fat handshaking stranger
in a red flannel suit
and a fake white beard   40
went around passing himself off
as some sort of North Pole saint
crossing the desert to Bethlehem
Pennsylvania
in a Volkswagon sled   45
drawn by rollicking Adirondack reindeer
with German names
and bearing sacks of Humble Gifts
from Saks Fifth Avenue
for everybody's imagined Christ child   50

Christ climbed down
from His bare Tree
this year
and ran away to where
no Bing Crosby carollers   55
groaned of a tight Christmas
and where no Radio City angels
iceskated wingless
thru a winter wonderland
into a jinglebell heaven   60
daily at 8:30
with Midnight Mass matinees

Christ climbed down
from His bare Tree
this year   65
and softly stole away into
some anonymous Mary's womb again
where in the darkest night
of everybody's anonymous soul
He awaits again   70
an unimaginable
and impossibly
Immaculate Reconception
the very craziest
of Second Comings   75

1. In "Signpost" what bearing has the allusion to "lilies of the field" on the poem? Show how the use of the imperative gives the poem a peculiarly dramatic quality.

2. Can you answer the questions asked in "Fog-Horn"? What is the effect of the continued questioning? Can you explain the phrases "something men had forgotten," "nearer than we had remembered," "something that we never meant"? Which do you think is the metaphor, the fog-horn or its double, the animal? What is the nature of the animal?

3. In "Christ Climbed Down" is there any way to relate Ferlinghetti's mention of a Second Coming with Yeats's poem of that name (page 8)?

The poems in the last group wrestle with the enormities of this century seen in wide or general terms. In the next poems the subject is more particularized: the violence and suffering have moved into our own streets and neighborhoods. The poem becomes a blow-up of actual incidents to which the poet bears witness.

Hearing Men Shout at Night on Macdougal Street

Robert Bly

How strange to awake in a city,
And hear grown men shouting in the night!
On the farm the darkness wins,
And the small ones nestle in their graves of cold:
Here is a boiling that only exhaustion subdues,   5
A bitter moiling of muddy waters
At which the voices of white men feed!

The street is a sea, and mud boils up
When the anchor is lifted, for now at midnight there
     is about to sail
The first New England slave-ship with the Negroes in
     the hold.   10

The Lowering

(Arlington Cemetery, June 8, 1968)

May Swenson

The
flag
is folded
lengthwise,
and lengthwise   5
again,

folding toward the
open edge,
so that the union of stars
on the blue   10
field remains outward in full view;

a triangular folding is then begun
at the striped end,
by bringing the corner of the folded edge
to the open edge;   15
the outer point, turned inward

along the open edge,
forms the next triangular fold;
the folding continued so, until the end is reached,
the final corner tucked between   20

the folds of the blue union,
the form of the folded flag

      is found to resemble that
      of a 3-cornered pouch, or thick cocked hat.
      Take this flag, John Glenn, instead of a friend;   25

instead of a brother, Edward
Kennedy, take this flag;

instead of a father, Joe
Kennedy, take this flag;
this flag instead of a husband, Ethel   30
Kennedy, take this flag;

this 9-times-folded
red-white-striped, star-spotted-blue flag,
tucked and pocketed neatly, Nation,
instead of a leader, take   35

this folded flag. Robert
Kennedy, coffin without coverlet,

beside this hole in the grass,
beside your brother, John
Kennedy, in the grass,   40
take, instead of a country,
this folded flag;
Robert

Kennedy, take
this hole   45
in the
grass.

Quaker Hero, Burning

Bink Noll

He erupts from our soil: a grenade
homemade out of outlandish parts
and tossed in a mad-man plot to split
the ground where officeholders talk.

He dwells in a furnace of concern,   5
in a monk cell worked by Consistency
in Truth's living rock, in a cave
where he dies a barbarian's wild death.

Though his mind's as clearly a man's mind
as his skull will remain a man's skull   10
when this thrill of incandescence
stops screaming at us from the smoke,

yet such blackness stuns the civil mind
with the same size as an act of God
that — while news comes of inhuman waste —   15
goes on beyond argument or aid.

Miners

James Wright

The police are dragging for the bodies
Of miners in the black waters
Of the suburbs.

Below, some few
Crawl, searching, until they clasp   5
The fingers of the sea.

Somewhere,
Beyond ripples and drowsing woodchucks,
A strong man, alone,
Beats on the door of a grave, crying   10
Oh let me in.

Many women mount long stairs
Into the shafts,
And emerge in the tottering palaces
Of abandoned cisterns.   15

In the middle of the night,
I can hear cars, moving on steel rails, colliding
Underground.

1. Discuss and compare the last five poems in regard to the following question: how has the horror of the event been communicated in the poem? that is, beyond the mere statement of fact, how have the poetic elements such as images, rhythm, and form intensified its reality?

2. How has the poet made a public act of violence into a personal experience in each case?

War is part of the consciousness, part of the living experience of this century. People are so used to it that they largely take it for granted. They think about it remotely, in abstract terms, until it forces itself on their personal lives. But the poet brings war close, out of a need to understand all he can of the reality of the times he lives in.

(Before beginning these poems you may want to refer back to the suggestions given on page 16 for reading a poem. However, it may be difficult to suppress such forceful images as these, as Miss Swenson suggests doing.)

There died a myriad

Ezra Pound

There died a myriad,
And of the best, among them,
For an old bitch gone in the teeth,
For a botched civilization,

Charm, smiling at the good mouth,   5
Quick eyes gone under earth's lid,

For two gross of broken statues,
For a few thousand battered books.

The Fury of Aerial Bombardment

Richard Eberhart

You would think the fury of aerial bombardment
Would rouse God to relent; the infinite spaces
Are still silent. He looks on shock-pried faces.
History, even, does not know what is meant.

You would feel that after so many centuries   5
God would give man to repent; yet he can kill
As Cain could, but with multitudinous will,
No farther advanced than in his ancient furies.

Was man made stupid to see his own stupidity?
Is God by definition indifferent, beyond us all?   10
Is the eternal truth man's fighting soul
Wherein the Beast ravens in its own avidity?

Of Van Wettering I speak, and Averill,
Names on a list, whose faces I do not recall
But they are gone to early death, who late in school   15
Distinguished the belt feed lever from the belt
      holding pawl.

The Raid

William Everson

They came out of the sun undetected,
Who had lain in the thin ships
All night long on the cold ocean,
Watched Vega* down, the Wain* hover,
Drank in the weakening dawn their brew,   5
And sent the lumbering death-laden birds
Level along the decks.

They came out of the sun with their guns geared,
Saw the soft and easy shape of that island
Laid on the sea,   10
An unwakening woman,
Its deep hollows and its flowing folds
Veiled in the garlands of its morning mists.
Each of them held in his aching eyes the erotic image,
And then tipped down,   15
In the target's trance,
In the ageless instant of the long descent,

4. Vega: *a brilliant white star in the constellation Lyra.* the Wain: *the Big Dipper.*

Pablo Picasso, *Guernica* (detail), on extended loan to The Museum of Modern Art, New York, from the artist.

And saw sweet chaos blossom below,
And felt in that flower the years release.

The perfect achievement.   20
They went back toward the sun crazy with joy,
Like wild birds weaving,
Drunkenly stunting;
Passed out over edge of that injured island,
Sought the rendezvous on the open sea   25
Where the ships would be waiting.

None were there.
Neither smoke nor smudge;
Neither spar nor splice nor rolling raft.
Only the wide waiting waste,   30
That each of them saw with intenser sight
Than he ever had spared it,
Who circled that spot,
The spent gauge caught in its final flutter,
And straggled down on their wavering wings   35
From the vast sky,
From the endless spaces,
Down at last for the low hover,
And the short quick quench of the sea.

A Camp in the Prussian Forest

Randall Jarrell

I walk beside the prisoners to the road.
Load on puffed load,
Their corpses, stacked like sodden wood,
Lie barred or galled with blood

By the charred warehouse. No one comes today   5
In the old way
To knock the fillings from their teeth;
The dark, coned, common wreath

Is plaited for their grave — a kind of grief.
The living leaf   10
Clings to the planted profitable
Pine if it is able;

The boughs sigh, mile on green, calm, breathing mile,
From this dead file
The planners ruled for them. . . . One year   15
They sent a million here:

Here men were drunk like water, burnt like wood.
The fat of good
And evil, the breast's star of hope*
Were rendered into soap.   20

I paint the star I sawed from yellow pine —
And plant the sign
In soil that does not yet refuse
Its usual Jews

Their first asylum. But the white, dwarfed star —   25
This dead white star* —
Hides nothing, pays for nothing; smoke
Fouls it, a yellow joke,

The needles of the wreath are chalked with ash,
A filmy trash   30

19. breast's star of hope: *the unfulfilled promise represented by the lives of those who were killed in the concentration camp. Also an allusion to the Star of David, a yellow, six-pointed star worn (frequently on the breast) by Jews in Nazi Germany.* 26. This dead white star: *earth.*

Litters the black woods with the death
Of men; and one last breath

Curls from the monstrous chimney. . . . I laugh aloud
Again and again;
The star laughs from its rotting shroud   35
Of flesh. O star* of men!

35–36. The star . . . star: *The many meanings of this symbol converge in these two lines.*

1. In each of the three last poems, an important change occurs in the last stanza. How has the rest of the poem led up to this change? What final blow is delivered at the end of each? How are rhythm and form wrenched by the force of the emotion, in each case?

2. Discuss the textural patterns in Pound's and Everson's poems — in particular the effects of the labials, the liquids, and the sibilants as they add to the meaning of the poem.

3. Do the great formality and abstractness of the Eberhart poem make it less emotionally forceful, or does the restraint of understatement give the poem even greater emotional power?

"It is impossible to write simply of what we know," one contemporary poet has said, of "the inhuman, unreal, smashing universe. . . ." Some poets, like the next two, have written very indirectly about war. The effect may be less shocking, but it is equally tragic.

The Third World

Lawrence Ferlinghetti

This loud morning
  sensed a small cry in
   the news
      paper
  caught somewhere on   5
   an inner page
       I
 decide to travel for lunch &
  end up in an automat
     White House Cafeteria 10
looking thru a little window
  put a nickel in the slot
   and out comes
       fried rice
   Taking a tour   15
  of the rest of that building
        I
     hear a small cry
  beyond the rice paddies
    between floors where 20
    the escalator sticks
and remember last night's dream of
  attending my own funeral
  at a drive-in mortuary
   not really believing   25
     I was that dead
   Someone throwing rice
      All the windows dry
 Tipped the coffin open & laughed
       into it   30
    and out falls
     old funnyface

>   myself
>   the bargain tragedian
>   with a small cry   35
> followed by sound of Che Guevara singing
>   in the voice of Fidel

>   Far over the Perfume River
>   the clouds pass
>   carrying small cries   40

>   The monsoon has set in
>   the windows weep
>   I
>   back up to
>   the Pentagon   45
>   on a flatbed truck
> and unload the small brown bodies
>   fresh from the blasted fields!

What Were They Like?

Denise Levertov

1) Did the people of Viet Nam
   use lanterns of stone?
2) Did they hold ceremonies
   to reverence the opening of buds?
3) Were they inclined to quiet laughter?   5
4) Did they use bone and ivory,
   jade and silver, for ornament?
5) Had they an epic poem?
6) Did they distinguish between speech and singing?

1) Sir, their light hearts turned to stone.   10
   It is not remembered whether in gardens

stone lanterns illumined pleasant ways.
2) Perhaps they gathered once to delight in blossom,
   but after the children were killed
   there were no more buds.   15
3) Sir, laughter is bitter to the burned mouth.
4) A dream ago, perhaps. Ornament is for joy.
   All the bones were charred.
5) It is not remembered. Remember,
   most were peasants; their life   20
   was in rice and bamboo.
   When peaceful clouds were reflected in the paddies
   and the water buffalo stepped surely along terraces,
   maybe fathers told their sons old tales.
   When bombs smashed those mirrors   25
   there was time only to scream.
6) There is an echo yet
   of their speech which was like a song.
   It was reported their singing resembled
   the flight of moths in moonlight.   30
   Who can say? It is silent now.

2

The Things of This World

"Love calls us to the things of this world," Richard Wilbur wrote (page 53) in a poem which celebrates the everyday world of things. Things, and especially those of nature, we know immediately through our senses. They are the reality which we all share — the source of all thought and memory and imagination. Poets have always written about nature as the ground of man's deepest experiences and understanding.

The natural world seems even more precious today as man discovers that he has already destroyed large parts of it. It is like a lost Eden that people try to return to — and in fact they do find happiness, in wilderness or city park, in being close to other living things. The nature poets of the nineteenth century assume a new relevance now, and some of the finest lyrical poems of the present time deal with man's ties to his first, and natural, world. One of the best of these, Dylan Thomas's "Fern Hill," recreates the joy of the poet's own boyhood experiences in the countryside of Wales:

Fern Hill

Dylan Thomas

Now as I was young and easy under the apple boughs
About the lilting house and happy as the grass was
      green,

The night above the dingle* starry,
    Time let me hail and climb
  Golden in the heydays of his eyes,   5
And honoured among wagons I was prince of the
      apple towns
And once below a time I lordly had the trees and
      leaves
    Trail with daisies and barley
  Down the rivers of the windfall light.

And as I was green and carefree, famous among the
      barns   10
About the happy yard and singing as the farm was
      home,
   In the sun that is young once only,
    Time let me play and be
  Golden in the mercy of his means,
And green and golden I was huntsman and herds-
      man, the calves   15
Sang to my horn, the foxes on the hills barked clear
      and cold,
    And the sabbath rang slowly
  In the pebbles of the holy streams.

All the sun long it was running, it was lovely, the hay
Fields high as the house, the tunes from the chimneys,
      it was air   20
    And playing, lovely and watery
      And fire green as grass.
    And nightly under the simple stars
As I rode to sleep the owls were bearing the farm
      away,
All the moon long I heard, blessed among stables, the
      nightjars*
        25

3. dingle: *small wooded valley.*
25. nightjars: *night birds.*

Flying with the ricks, and the horses
    Flashing into the dark.

And then to awake, and the farm, like a wanderer
    white
With the dew, come back, the cock on his shoulder:
    it was all
    Shining, it was Adam and maiden,   30
      The sky gathered again
    And the sun grew round that very day.
So it must have been after the birth of the simple light
In the first, spinning place, the spellbound horses
    walking warm
    Out of the whinnying green stable   35
      On to the fields of praise.

And honoured among foxes and pheasants by the gay
    house
Under the new made clouds and happy as the heart
    was long,
    In the sun born over and over,
      I ran my heedless ways,   40
    My wishes raced through the house high hay
And nothing I cared, at my sky blue trades, that time
    allows
In all his tuneful turning so few and such morning
    songs
    Before the children green and golden
      Follow him out of grace,   45
Nothing I cared, in the lamb white days, that time
    would take me
Up to the swallow thronged loft by the shadow of my
    hand,
    In the moon that is always rising,
      Nor that riding to sleep
    I should hear him fly with the high fields   50

And wake to the farm forever fled from the childless
            land.
Oh as I was young and easy in the mercy of his means,
        Time held me green and dying
    Though I sang in my chains like the sea.

1. A highly individual poet, Dylan Thomas is known for the extra-ordinary music of his poetry. This can be appreciated by hearing the poet read his own works (Caedmon TC 1002). However, by reading the poem aloud, you can discover the lyric quality. What changes of mood do you hear in it? where?

2. Is the counter theme of sadness in conflict with the dominant mood of the poem, or are the two easily harmonized into the child's world? The music and the images of the poem should provide a clue: are there discords that suggest a tension between the two moods? (What is the cause of the sadness?)

3. The phrasing in this poem is often surprising — with replacements such as "once below a time"; with odd liaisons of association in phrases like "windfall light" and in lines like "And the sabbath rang slowly / In the pebbles of the holy streams." What is the special power of such language? Find other examples and comment on them.

Man's own origin and his relation to the universe have been constant questions throughout history. People turned to the many myths of creation, the work of ancient poets and prophets, for the answer to these questions. In a scientific age, the theory of evolution is our answer — an answer no less marvelous than earlier poetic theories. The miracle of life and evolution is the subject of the following three poems.

Continent's End

Robinson Jeffers

At the equinox when the earth was veiled in a late
    rain, wreathed with wet poppies, waiting spring,
The ocean swelled for a far storm and beat its bound-
    ary, the ground-swell shook the beds of granite:
I gazing at the boundaries of granite and spray, the   5
    established sea-marks, felt behind me
Mountain and plain, the immense breadth of the con-
    tinent, before me the mass and doubled stretch
    of water.
I said: You yoke the Aleutian seal-rocks with the lava
    and coral sowings that flower the south,   10
Over your flood the life that sought the sunrise faces
    ours that has followed the evening star.
The long migrations meet across you and it is nothing
    to you, you have forgotten us, mother.
You were much younger when we crawled out of the   15
    womb and lay in the sun's eye on the tideline.
It was long and long ago; we have grown proud since
    then and you have grown bitter; life retains
Your mobile soft unquiet strength; and envies hard-
    ness, the insolent quietness of stone.   20
The tides are in our veins, we still mirror the stars,
    life is your child, but there is in me
Older and harder than life and more impartial, the
    eye that watched before there was an ocean.
That watched you fill your beds out of the condensa-   25
    tion of thin vapor and watched you change them,
That saw you soft and violent wear your boundaries
    down, eat rock, shift places with the continents.
Mother, though my song's measure is like your surf-
    beat's ancient rhythm I never learned it of you.   30
Before there was any water there were tides of fire,
    both our tones flow from the older fountain.

Evolution

May Swenson

the stone
would like to be
Alive like me

the rooted tree
longs to be Free

the mute beast
envies my fate
Articulate

on this ball
half dark
half light
i walk Upright
i lie Prone
within the night

beautiful each Shape
to see
wonderful each Thing
to name
here a stone
there a tree
here a river
there a Flame

marvelous to Stroke
the patient beasts
within their yoke

How i Yearn
for the lion
in his den
though he spurn
the touch of men

the longing
that i know
is in the Stone also
it must be

the same that rises
in the Tree
the longing
in the Lion's call
speaks for all

oh to Endure
like the stone
sufficient
to itself alone

or Reincarnate
like the tree
be born each spring
to greenery

or like the lion
without law
to roam the Wild
on velvet paw

but if walking
i meet
a Creature like me
on the street
two-legged
with human face
to recognize
is to Embrace

wonders pale
beauties dim
during my delight
with Him

an Evolution strange
two Tongues touch
exchange
a Feast unknown
to stone
or tree or beast

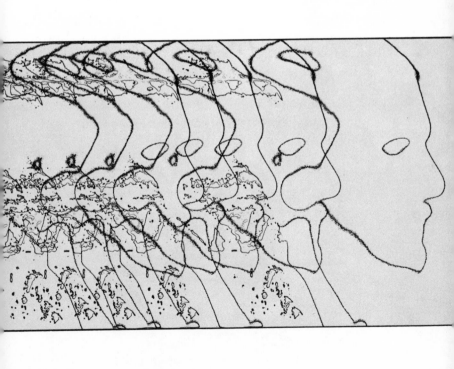

MONET: "Les Nymphéas"

W. D. Snodgrass

The eyelids glowing, some chill morning.
O world half-known through opening, twilit lids
  Before the vague face clenches into light;
O universal waters like a cloud,
  Like those first clouds of half-created matter;   5
O all things rising, rising like the fumes
  From waters falling, O forever falling;
Infinite, the skeletal shells that fall, relinquished,
  The snowsoft sift of the diatoms,* like selves
Downdrifting age upon age through milky oceans;   10
  O slow downdrifting of the atoms;
O island nebulae and O the nebulous islands
  Wandering these mists like falsefires, which are
      true,
Bobbing like milkweed, like warm lanterns bobbing
  Through the snowfilled windless air, blinking and
      passing   15
As we pass into the memory of women
  Who are passing. Within those depths
What ravening? What devouring rage?
  How shall our living know its ends of yielding?
These things have taken me as the mouth an orange — 20
  That acrid sweet juice entering every cell;
And I am shared out. I become these things:
  These lilies, if these things are water lilies

"Les Nymphéas": *the water lily paintings of the French impressionist Claude Monet, which concentrate upon the reflection of light and color as perceived through water.*
9. diatoms: *microscopic algae.*

Which are dancers growing dim across no floor;
   These mayflies; whirled dust orbiting in the sun;   25
This blossoming diffused as rushlights; galactic
     vapors;
   Fluorescence into which we pass and penetrate;
O soft as the thighs of women;
   O radiance, into which I go on dying . . .

1. How does the speaker in each poem view the theory of evolution? What statement does each poem seem to be making about it? In each, how is human proportion brought into the vast scale of evolutionary time?

2. What themes, other than the main subject of evolution, do you find in each of these poems? Show how different kinds of images are linked through theme. For example, in the Snodgrass poem the speaker, the woman, the diatoms, and the galaxies are brought together from disparate realms of experience. How are they meshed?

   What purpose is served by the many *-ing* words in this poem?

3. Symmetry of form is conspicuous in all three of these poems. How does it strengthen the meaning of each poem? Which poem do you think is most successful in relating form to the development of the different themes? In which does the musical element of the poem seem to be most successful?

But man has responded to nature in more than speculative ways. He has always pitted himself against her: at first for survival, then later for a unique kind of pleasure and exhilaration that are only heightened by danger. The two poems that follow capture the skill and drama of man's sports.

Skiers

To Baudouin and Annie de Moustier

Robert Penn Warren

With the motion of angels, out of
Snow-spume and swirl of gold mist, they
Emerge to the positive sun. At
That great height, small on that whiteness,
With the color of birds or of angels,   5
They swoop, sway, descend, and descending,
Cry their bright bird-cries, pure
In the sweet desolation of distance.
They slowly enlarge to our eyes. Now

On the flat where the whiteness is   10
Trodden and mud-streaked, not birds now,
Nor angels even, they stand. They

Are awkward, not yet well adjusted
To this world, new and strange, of Time and
Contingency, who now are only   15
Human. They smile. The human

Face has its own beauty.

John Muir on Mt. Ritter

Gary Snyder

John Muir* on Mt. Ritter:

After scanning its face again and again,
I/began to scale it, picking my holds
With intense caution. About half-way
To the top, I was suddenly brought to   5
A dead stop, with arms outspread
Clinging close to the face of the rock
Unable to move hand or foot
Either up or down. My doom
Appeared fixed. I MUST fall.   10
There would be a moment of
Bewilderment, and then,
A lifeless rumble down the cliff
To the glacier below.
My mind seemed to fill with a   15
Stifling smoke. This terrible eclipse
Lasted only a moment, when life blazed
Forth again with preternatural clearness.
I seemed suddenly to become possessed
Of a new sense. My trembling muscles   20
Became firm again, every rift and flaw in
The rock was seen as through a microscope,
My limbs moved with a positiveness and precision
With which I seemed to have
Nothing at all to do.   25

1. John Muir: *an American naturalist of the nineteenth and early twentieth
centuries, who described his extensive wanderings in such books as* The
Mountains of California *and* My First Summer in the Sierra.

1. Both poems are quite free in form. As you read them aloud, however, what kinds of rhythms and form emerge?

2. Comment on the effectiveness of the last line of each of the preceding poems.

Man-made things can stir lyrical feelings too, for they are often beautiful or affecting. But even here, it is often the natural world that supplies the poet with images. The next poems show the poet in a playful mood, delighted with the things that men have made.

Don't let that horse

Lawrence Ferlinghetti

Don't let that horse
                    eat that violin

   cried Chagall's* mother

                        But he
              kept right on   5
                        painting

And became famous

And kept on painting
                    The Horse With Violin In Mouth

---

3. Chagall: *Marc Chagall is a French painter whose fanciful and dreamlike art often incorporates images from his childhood in Russia. The violin is a recurring motif in his paintings.*

And when he finally finished it   10
he jumped up upon the horse
                              and rode away
          waving the violin

And then with a low bow gave it
to the first naked nude he ran across   15

And there were no strings
                    attached

In the second-best hotel in Tokyo

Karl Shapiro

In the second-best hotel in Tokyo the chambermaids
are chasing the chamberboys. Laughter tinkles
up and down the halls. The elevator girls sing it
when they say: ten floor, please; seven floor,
please (their faces like gardenias). The cashier's   5
fingers race back and forth over the counting
frame.

In the first-best Western-style hotel in Kyoto I describe to the barmaid how to make a Bloody
Mary, and am proud. I walk through the fish
market with the editor of *The Kenyon Review.*   10
The fishes are displayed like masterpieces. This
is more beautiful than the Louvre.*

I fall in love with the torii gate,* graceful salmon arms,
the light rust color. From now on it's my Par-
thenon. The wooden golden palace floats on its   15
pond. The nightingale floors warn me of my
assassins. I sleep like an Oriental.

Zen is on the verge of being discovered. We climb to
the famous abstract garden and study the sand
designs and the rocks. To my companion I say: 20
how do they fix it without messing it up? He
laughs at my westernization.

As for the haiku,* you can make it tough. It isn't
exactly a valentine, except in the States.

12. the Louvre: *Paris art museum, one of the world's most famous.*
13. torii gate: *decorative gate to Shinto temple.*
23. haiku: *seventeen-syllable Japanese poem which relies on image, concentration, and precision for its effects.*

The 59th Street Bridge Song
Feelin' Groovy

Paul Simon

Slow down,
You move too fast.
You got to make the morning last.
Just kickin' down the cobblestones,
Lookin' for fun and Feelin' Groovy.   5

Hello lamppost,
What-cha knowin'
I've come to watch your flowers growin'.
Ain't-cha got no rhymes for me?
Doot'in' doo-doo, Feelin' Groovy.   10

Got no deeds to do,
No promises to keep.
I'm dappled and drowsy and ready to sleep.
Let the morningtime drop all its petals on me.
Life, I love you.   15
All is Groovy.

1. The paintings of Chagall are characteristically full of fantasy. What
    else does "Don't let that horse" suggest about Chagall's art?
    What two levels of reality run together in this poem? What does
    this tell about the nature of art (and poetry) as Ferlinghetti sees it?

2. What does the Shapiro poem suggest about the feeling of the
    Japanese experience? (Pictures of Japanese gardens and the torii
    gate may help here.) Does the colloquial tone of the language and
    its prose-like form interfere with the poem's lyrical quality?
    Show how the last two lines bring together Shapiro's idea of art
    and the difference between Japanese awareness and American.

Love Calls Us to the Things
of This World

Richard Wilbur

The eyes open to a cry of pulleys,
And spirited from sleep, the astounded soul
Hangs for a moment bodiless and simple
As false dawn.
                      Outside the open window   5
The morning air is all awash with angels.

Some are in bed-sheets, some are in blouses,
Some are in smocks: but truly there they are.
Now they are rising together in calm swells
Of halcyon* feeling, filling whatever they wear   10
With the deep joy of their impersonal breathing;

Now they are flying in place, conveying
The terrible speed of their omnipresence, moving
And staying like white water; and now of a sudden
They swoon down into so rapt a quiet   15
That nobody seems to be there.
                                The soul shrinks

From all that it is about to remember,
From the punctual rape of every blessèd day,
And cries,   20
            "Oh, let there be nothing on earth but
                laundry,
Nothing but rosy hands in the rising steam
And clear dances done in the sight of heaven."

---

10. halcyon: *calm. The halcyon bird, according to legend, nested at sea and calmed the waves during the incubation period.*

Yet, as the sun acknowledges
With a warm look the world's hunks and colors,   25
The soul descends once more in bitter love
To accept the waking body, saying now
In a changed voice as the man yawns and rises,

"Bring them down from their ruddy gallows;
Let there be clean linen for the backs of thieves;   30
Let lovers go fresh and sweet to be undone,
And the heaviest nuns walk in a pure floating
Of dark habits,
                keeping their difficult balance."

1. Comment on the use of the word "angels" in line 6. Does it seem
    paradoxical? How do the "things of this world" appear to the
    speaker's awakening consciousness?

2. From what does the soul shrink (line 17)? What is the conflict
    here, and how is it resolved in the last stanza? What part does love
    play?

3. Notice the surprising juxtapositions of words, as in "the punctual
    rape of every blessèd day." Can you find others? What special
    quality do they give the poem?

4. How are the sound and the shifting rhythms related to the progres-
    sion of thought in the poem?

The term *nature poem* is apt to suggest a sentimental approach
to life and poetry. However, the next three poems, though their
subject is nature in different facets, each develop a clear and
vigorous quality, grounded upon closest observation.

Again, in reading, you may want to follow the procedure suggested on page 16: read first for sound, then for shape, and finally
for images.

Spring Pools

Robert Frost

These pools that, though in forests, still reflect
The total sky almost without defect,
And like the flowers beside them, chill and shiver,
Will like the flowers beside them soon be gone,
And yet not out by any brook or river,   5
But up by roots to bring dark foliage on.

The trees that have it in their pent-up buds
To darken nature and be summer woods —
Let them think twice before they use their powers
To blot out and drink up and sweep away   10
These flowery waters and these watery flowers
From snow that melted only yesterday.

Spring and All

William Carlos Williams

I

By the road to the contagious hospital⁻
under the surge of the blue
mottled clouds driven from the
northeast — a cold wind. Beyond, the
waste of broad, muddy fields   5
brown with dried weeds, standing and fallen

patches of standing water
the scattering of tall trees

All along the road the reddish
purplish, forked, upstanding, twiggy   10

stuff of bushes and small trees
with dead, brown leaves under them
leafless vines —

Lifeless in appearance, sluggish
dazed spring approaches —   15

They enter the new world naked,
cold, uncertain of all
save that they enter. All about them
the cold, familiar wind —

Now the grass, tomorrow   20
the stiff curl of wildcarrot leaf

One by one objects are defined —
It quickens: clarity, outline of leaf

But now the stark dignity of
entrance — Still, the profound change   25
has come upon them: rooted they
grip down and begin to awaken

II

Pink confused with white
flowers and flowers reversed
take and spill the shaded flame   30
darting it back
into the lamp's horn

petals aslant darkened with mauve

red where in whorls
petal lays its glow upon petal   35
round flamegreen throats

petals radiant with transpiercing light
contending
        above
the leaves   40
reaching up their modest green
from the pot's rim

and there, wholly dark, the pot
gay with rough moss.

The Wild Swans at Coole

William Butler Yeats

The trees are in their autumn beauty,
The woodland paths are dry,
Under the October twilight the water
Mirrors a still sky;
Upon the brimming water among the stones   5
Are nine-and-fifty swans.

The nineteenth autumn has come upon me
Since I first made my count;
I saw, before I had well finished,
All suddenly mount   10
And scatter wheeling in great broken rings
Upon their clamorous wings.

I have looked upon those brilliant creatures,
And now my heart is sore.
All's changed since I, hearing at twilight,   15
The first time on this shore,
The bell-beat of their wings above my head,
Trod with a lighter tread.

Unwearied still, lover by lover,
They paddle in the cold   20
Companionable streams or climb the air;
Their hearts have not grown old;
Passion or conquest, wander where they will,
Attend upon them still.

But now they drift on the still water,   25
Mysterious, beautiful;
Among what rushes will they build,
By what lake's edge or pool
Delight men's eyes when I awake some day
To find they have flown away?   30

1. What is the paradox of waters that Frost describes? Notice how the struggle is underscored by the harsh consonants which obstruct the flow of lines 5–6 and 9–10.

2. Contrast the consonance (repetition of the final consonant in the stressed syllable of words) of Williams's poem with that of Frost. Is the difference in the sounds important to the images that the words call up?

3. Both Williams and Frost have a strong empathic response to nature; both have the faculty of entering into a life that is unlike man's and of giving it powerful expression. Sometimes they bring a sense of primal forces that chill with menace. Do you find a trace of that in either of these poems? Explain.

4. Like the poetry of the Welsh poet Dylan Thomas, that of Yeats, who was Irish, reflects the strong musical quality of Celtic speech. How does the tone of "The Wild Swans at Coole" compare with either of the other two poems in this group? In what other ways does it differ? What, for instance, is the relationship between the speaker and the swans? How do you understand the question at the end of the poem?

Though modern man has subdued nature in many ways, yet alone and without his technological armor he can still feel its menace and power — as the following poems show. It is hard for most people not to anthropomorphize animals, hard to see them in anything but human terms. (Spiders are cruel, lambs innocent, for example, are sentimental judgments.) These poems make an effort to understand animals as they are in themselves, to discover the "otherness" of nonhuman beings.

Leviathan

W. S. Merwin

This is the black sea-brute bulling through wave-
    wrack,
Ancient as ocean's shifting hills, who in sea-toils
Travelling, who furrowing the salt acres
Heavily, his wake hoary behind him,
Shoulders spouting, the fist of his forehead   5
Over wastes gray-green crashing, among horses
    unbroken
From bellowing fields, past bone-wreck of vessels,
Tide-ruin, wash of lost bodies bobbing
No longer sought for, and islands of ice gleaming,
Who ravening the rank flood, wave-marshalling,   10
Overmastering the dark sea-marches, finds home
And harvest. Frightening to foolhardiest
Mariners, his size were difficult to describe:
The hulk of him is like hills heaving,
Dark, yet as crags of drift-ice, crowns cracking in
    thunder,   15
Like land's self by night black-looming, surf churning
    and trailing
Along his shores' rushing, shoal-water boding

About the dark of his jaws; and who should moor at
    his edge
And fare on afoot would find gates of no gardens,
But the hill of dark underfoot diving,   20
Closing overhead, the cold deep, and drowning.
He is called Leviathan, and named for rolling,*
First created he was of all creatures,
He has held Jonah three days and nights,
He is that curling serpent that in ocean is,   25
Sea-fright he is, and the shadow under the earth.
Days there are, nonetheless, when he lies
Like an angel, although a lost angel
On the waste's unease, no eye of man moving,
Bird hovering, fish flashing, creature whatever   30
Who after him came to herit earth's emptiness.
Froth at flanks seething sooths to stillness,
Waits; with one eye he watches
Dark of night sinking last, with one eye dayrise
As at first over foaming pastures. He makes no cry   35
Though that light is a breath. The sea curling,
Star-climbed, wind-combed, cumbered with itself still
As at first it was, is the hand not yet contented
Of the Creator. And he waits for the world to begin.

22. named for rolling: *The Hebrew name probably means "the coiling up."*

Birds and Fishes

Robinson Jeffers

Every October millions of little fish come along the
    shore,
Coasting this granite edge of the continent

On their lawful occasions: but what a festival for the
    seafowl.
What a witches' sabbath of wings
Hides the dark water. The heavy pelicans shout
    "Haw!" like Job's friend's warhorse   5
And dive from the high air, the cormorants
Slip their long black bodies under the water and hunt
    like wolves
Through the green half-light. Screaming, the gulls
    watch,
Wild with envy and malice, cursing and snatching.
    What hysterical greed!
What a filling of pouches! the mob   10
Hysteria is nearly human — these decent birds! — as
    if they were finding
Gold in the street. It is better than gold,
It can be eaten: and which one in all this fury of wild-
    fowl pities the fish?
No one certainly. Justice and mercy
Are human dreams, they do not concern the birds nor
    the fish nor eternal God.   15
However — look again before you go.
The wings and the wild hungers, the wave-worn
    skerries,* the bright quick minnows
Living in terror to die in torment —
Man's fate and theirs — and the island rocks and im-
    mense ocean beyond, and Lobos
Darkening above the bay: they are beautiful?   20
That is their quality: not mercy, not mind, not good-
    ness, but the beauty of God.

17. skerries: *reefs.*

The Trees

William Carlos Williams

The trees — being trees
thrash and scream
guffaw and curse —
wholly abandoned
damning the race of men —   5

Christ, the bastards
haven't even sense enough
to stay out of the rain —

Wha ha ha ha

Wheeeeee   10
Clacka tacka tacka
tacka tacka
wha ha ha ha ha
ha ha ha

knocking knees, buds   15
bursting from each pore
even the trunk's self
putting out leafheads —

Loose desire!
we naked cry to you —   20
"Do what you please."

You cannot!

— ghosts
sapped of strength

wailing at the gate   25
heartbreak at the bridgehead —

desire
dead in the heart

haw haw haw haw
— and memory broken   30

wheeeeee

There were never satyrs*
never maenads*
never eagle-headed gods —
These were men   35
from whose hands sprung
love
bursting the wood —

Trees their companions
— a cold wind winterlong   40
in the hollows of our flesh
icy with pleasure —

no part of us untouched

32. satyrs: *creatures from Greek mythology, half horse, half man.*
33. maenads: *woman followers of the god Bacchus.*

The Heaven of Animals

James Dickey

Here they are. The soft eyes open.
If they have lived in a wood
It is a wood.
If they have lived on plains
It is grass rolling   5
Under their feet forever.

Having no souls, they have come,
Anyway, beyond their knowing.
Their instincts wholly bloom
And they rise.   10
The soft eyes open.

To match them, the landscape flowers,
Outdoing, desperately
Outdoing what is required:
The richest wood,   15
The deepest field.

For some of these,
It could not be the place
It is, without blood.
These hunt, as they have done,   20
But with claws and teeth grown perfect,

More deadly than they can believe.
They stalk more silently,
And crouch on the limbs of trees,
And their descent   25
Upon the bright backs of their prey

May take years
In a sovereign floating of joy.

And those that are hunted
Know this as their life,   30
Their reward: to walk

Under such trees in full knowledge
Of what is in glory above them,
And to feel no fear,
But acceptance, compliance.   35
Fulfilling themselves without pain

At the cycle's center,
They tremble, they walk
Under the tree,
They fall, they are torn,   40
They rise, they walk again.

The next two poems show an acute awareness that the natural world is irreplaceable, unique among the galaxies, and that it must be cherished and preserved.

Deer Among Cattle

James Dickey

Here and there in the searing beam
Of my hand going through the night meadow
They all are grazing

With pins of human light in their eyes.
A wild one also is eating   5
The human grass,

Slender, graceful, domesticated
By darkness, among the bred-
for-slaughter,

Having bounded their paralyzed fence   10
And inclined his branched forehead onto
Their green frosted table,

The only live thing in this flashlight
Who can leave whenever he wishes,
Turn grass into forest,   15

Foreclose inhuman brightness from his eyes
But stands here still, unperturbed,
In their wide-open country,

The sparks from my hand in his pupils
Unmatched anywhere among cattle,   20

Grazing with them the night of the hammer
As one of their own who shall rise.

The Breathing

Denise Levertov

An absolute
patience.
Trees stand
up to their knees in
fog. The fog   5
slowly flows
uphill.
        White
cobwebs, the grass
leaning where deer   10
have looked for apples.
The woods

from brook to where
the top of the hill looks
over the fog, send up   15
not one bird.
So absolute, it is
no other than
happiness itself, a breathing
too quiet to hear.   20

3

Love

The Greeks divided love into three kinds: *eros,* sexual love; *philia,* love for family and friends; and *agape,* a love for every human being, especially those in need. Today, if we take the advertisements seriously, *eros,* or romantic love, takes precedence over everything and seems to be the end-all of existence: strange to remember that the Greeks thought of it as a kind of madness, fortunately not very long-lasting! *Philia* happens to most people naturally: families grow up affectionately, or we find congenial friends outside. But *agape,* the most demanding, suffers neglect. Selfishness stands in the way, and it takes a generosity of spirit to embrace strangers whose ways are not our ways.

Love, in all its forms, has been a constant subject for poetry. Today's poets too write about this oldest, and most humanizing, of human experiences — and find fresh language to express it.

Sometimes a perfectly simple poem about love can hold worlds:

For Anne

Leonard Cohen

With Annie gone,
Whose eyes to compare
With the morning sun?

Not that I did compare,
But I do compare   5
Now that she's gone.

Father and Child

William Butler Yeats

She hears me strike the board and say
That she is under ban
Of all good men and women,
Being mentioned with a man
That has the worst of all bad names;   5
And thereupon replies
That his hair is beautiful,
Cold as the March wind his eyes.

A Deep-Sworn Vow

William Butler Yeats

Others because you did not keep
That deep-sworn vow have been friends of mine;

Yet always when I look death in the face,
When I clamber to the heights of sleep,
Or when I grow excited with wine,   5
Suddenly I meet your face.

1. In these tiny dramas, how do the strong end-rhymes and the rhythms generate both feeling and movement?
2. In each poem, how do both climax and surprise happen within so short a space?

Sometimes quite complex poems, because of their intensity, can seem like simple and spontaneous expressions of love.

if everything happens that can't be done

E. E. Cummings

if everything happens that can't be done
(and anything's righter
than books
could plan)
the stupidest teacher will almost guess   5
(with a run
skip
around we go yes)
there's nothing as something as one

one hasn't a why or because or although   10
(and buds know better

than books
don't grow)
one's anything old being everything new
(with a what   15
which
around we come who)
one's everyanything so

so world is a leaf so tree is a bough
(and birds sing sweeter   20
than books
tell how)
so here is away and so your is a my
(with a down
up   25
around again fly)
forever was never till now

now i love you and you love me
(and books are shuter
than books   30
can be)
and deep in the high that does nothing but fall
(with a shout
each
around we go all)   35
there's somebody calling who's we

we're anything brighter than even the sun
(we're everything greater
than books
might mean)   40
we're everyanything more than believe
(with a spin
leap
alive we're alive)
we're wonderful one times one   45

Song

Robert Creeley

What do you
want, love. To be
loved. What,

what wanted,
love, wanted   5
so much as love

like nothing
considered, no
feeling but

a simple   10
recognition
forgotten sits

in its feeling,
two things,
one and one.   15

1. Read the Cummings poem (page 72) aloud several times, giving
   emphasis to its dance-like rhythm. Which phrases further suggest
   the idea of a dance?

2. The pattern of this poem on the page and the typography are part of
   the meaning. What single theme is developed in the first parenthesis in each stanza? In what way does the second parenthesis
   of each stanza suggest a stage direction?

3. The first, middle, and last lines in each stanza are almost all
   paradoxes. How do these prepare for the finale of the last line? —
   and how does the last line help resolve the earlier paradoxes?

4. How is the structure of the ideas in this poem followed in the line
   patterns, the changing rhythms, the punctuation, and the extreme

symmetry? What is the poet's purpose in using lower case letters throughout, unconventional punctuation, and unusual syntax?

5. Read the Creeley poem aloud, making a perceptible pause at the end of each line. This will emphasize the integrity of the line as a unit, in a kind of counterpoint to the larger meanings of the sentence and of the whole poem.

   What special feeling do you find in the spareness of the language? the absence of concrete images? the short, seemingly broken lines? the questions that seem to answer themselves? What is the relation of the words, often repeated, to the movement of the poem? Notice how the syntax, as it moves, creates the form of this poem.

W. H. Auden said once that he was always interested in "what kind of guy" wrote the poem he was reading. What can you tell about the authors of the next poems? One cannot, of course, assume that the speaker in a poem and the author are identical, even when the poem seems clearly autobiographical. But the poet always reveals many things about himself, by his characteristic phrasing and images, as well as by his subject and the values he implies.

In spite of their differences, these next three love poems all have a specifically twentieth-century quality. Can you describe it?

Summer Night

Leonard Cohen

The moon dangling wet like a half-plucked eye
was bright for my friends bred in close avenues
of stone, and let us see too much.
The vast treeless field and huge wounded sky,
opposing each other like continents,   5

made us and our smoking fire quite irrelevant
between their eternal attitudes.
We knew we were intruders. Worse. Intruders
unnoticed and undespised.
   Through orchards of black weeds   10
with a sigh the river urged its silver flesh.
From their damp nests bull-frogs croaked
warnings, but to each other.
And occasional birds, in a private grudge,
flew noiselessly at the moon.   15
What could we do? We ran naked into the river,
but our flesh insulted the thick slow water.
We tried to sit naked on the stones,
but they were cold and we soon dressed.
One squeezed a little human music from his box: 20
mostly it was lost in the grass
where one struggled in an ignorant embrace.
One argued with the slight old hills
and the goose-fleshed naked girls, I will not be old.
One, for his protest, registered a sexual groan.   25
And the girl in my arms
broke suddenly away, and shouted for us all,
Help! Help! I am alone. But then all subtlety was
    gone
and it was stupid to be obvious before the field and
    sky,
experts in simplicity. So we fled on the highways,   30
in our armoured cars, back to air-conditioned homes.

Love Poem

John Frederick Nims

My clumsiest dear, whose hands shipwreck vases,
At whose quick touch all glasses chip and ring,

Whose palms are bulls in china, burs in linen,
And have no cunning with any soft thing

Except all ill at ease fidgeting people: 5
The refugee uncertain at the door
You make at home; deftly you steady
The drunk clambering on his undulant floor.

Unpredictable dear, the taxi drivers' terror,
Shrinking from far headlights pale as a dime   10
Yet leaping before red apoplectic streetcars —
Misfit in any space. And never on time.

A wrench in clocks and the solar system. Only
With words and people and love you move at ease.
In traffic of wit expertly manoeuvre   15
And keep us, all devotion, at your knees.

Forgetting your coffee spreading on our flannel,
Your lipstick grinning on our coat,
So gayly in love's unbreakable heaven
Our souls on glory of spilt bourbon float.   20

Be with me darling early and late. Smash glasses —
I will study wry music for your sake.
For should your hands drop white and empty
All the toys of the world would break.

I Knew a Woman

Theodore Roethke

I knew a woman, lovely in her bones,
When small birds sighed, she would sigh back at
     them;

Ah, when she moved, she moved more ways than one:
The shapes a bright container can contain!
Of her choice virtues only gods should speak,   5
Or English poets who grew up on Greek
(I'd have them sing in chorus, cheek to cheek).

How well her wishes went! She stroked my chin,
She taught me Turn, and Counter-turn, and Stand;
She taught me Touch, that undulant white skin;   10
I nibbled meekly from her proffered hand;
She was the sickle; I, poor I, the rake,
Coming behind her for her pretty sake
(But what prodigious mowing we did make).

Love likes a gander, and adores a goose: 15
Her full lips pursed, the errant note to seize;
She played it quick, she played it light and loose;
My eyes, they dazzled at her flowing knees;
Her several parts could keep a pure repose,
Or one hip quiver with a mobile nose   20
(She moved in circles, and those circles moved).

Let seed be grass, and grass turn into hay:
I'm martyr to a motion not my own;
What's freedom for? To know eternity.
I swear she cast a shadow white as stone.   25
But who would count eternity in days?
These old bones live to learn her wanton ways:
(I measure time by how a body sways).

Poets have also written of the special love that parents feel for their children — of their hope that the child will find fulfillment and of the pain of separation as the child grows away from them. Or, occasionally, of how the love for a child can sustain a parent when all other hope is gone.

The Name

Robert Creeley

Be natural
wise
as you can be,
my daughter,

let my name   5
be in you flesh
I gave you
in the act of

loving your mother,
all your days   10
her ways,
the woman in you

brought from
sensuality's measure
no other,   15
there was no thought

of it but such
pleasure all women
must be in her,
as you. But not wiser,   20

not more of nature
than her hair,
the eyes
she gives you.

There will not be another   25
woman such as you

are. Remember
your mother,

the way you came,
the days of waiting.   30
Be natural,
daughter, wise

as you can be,
all my daughters,
be women   35
for men

when that time comes.
Let the rhetoric
stay with me
your father. Let   40

me talk about it,
saving you such
vicious self-
exposure, let you

pass it on   45
in you. I cannot
be more than the man
who watches.

On Giving a Son to the Sea

James Dickey

Gentle blondness and the moray eel go at the same time
On in my mind as you grow, who fired at me, at the age
    Of six, a Christmas toy for child

Spies   a bullet with a Special Secret
Message Compartment. My hands undid the bullet meant   5
      For my heart, and it read aloud
    "I love you." That message hits me most
When I watch you swim, that being your only talent.
The sea obsesses you, and your room is full of it:

      Your room is full   10
    Of flippers and snorkels and books
    On spearfishing.
              O the depths,
My gentle son. Out of that room and into the real
      Wonder and weightless horror   15
  Of water   into the shifts of vastness
You will probably go, for someone must lead
    Mankind, your father and your sons,
    Down there to live, or we all die
      Of crowding. Many of you   20
      Will die, in the cold roll
  Of the bottom currents, and the life lost
More totally than anywhere, there in the dark
Of no breath at all.
            And I must let you go, out of your gentle   25
    Childhood into your own man suspended
    In its body, slowly waving its feet
Deeper and deeper, while the dark grows, the cold
    Grows careless, the sun is put
      Out by the weight of the planet   30
As it sinks to the bottom. Maybe you will find us there
An agonizing new life, much like the life
Of the drowned, where we will farm eat sleep and bear
    children
  Who dream of birds.
          Switch on your sea-lamp then,   35
And go downward, son, with your only message
Echoing.   Your message to the world, remember,
    Came to your father

At Christmas like a bullet.   When the great fish roll
    With you, herded deep in the deepest dance,   40
  When the shark cuts through your invisible
        Trail, I will send back
That message, though nothing that lives
     Underwater will ever receive it.
     That does not matter, my gentle blond   45
    Son.   That does not matter.

Preface to a Twenty Volume
Suicide Note

LeRoi Jones

Lately, I've become accustomed to the way
The ground opens up and envelops me
Each time I go out to walk the dog.
Or the broad edged silly music the wind
Makes when I run for a bus —   5

Things have come to that.

And now, each night I count the stars,
And each night I get the same number.
And when they will not come to be counted
I count the holes they leave.   10

Nobody sings anymore.

And then last night, I tiptoed up
To my daughter's room and heard her
Talking to someone, and when I opened
The door, there was no one there . . .   15
Only she on her knees,
Peeking into her own clasped hands.

1. Compare the fathers in the last three poems in terms of their relationship to their children. Have they anything in common?

2. Robert Creeley wrote about "The Name," "I like the way this poem moves, in its lines, in the way certain words pick up echoes of rhymes in others. . . . I like the syncopation of the rhythms. . . . I feel poetry as a complex of sounds and rhythms (and) it is just this complex that makes poetry be the very singular *fact* of words which it is." Can you apply these remarks to "The Name"? What does Creeley mean by poetry being a very singular "*fact* of words"?

3. In "On Giving a Son to the Sea," what does the extended metaphor tell you about the relationship of the father and the son? What great hopes has the father for his son? What does the father believe is his son's "message to the world," and what is its connection to Christmas? The images of the many undersea dangers suggest that the sea itself is a symbol in this poem: of what?

4. In LeRoi Jones's poem, trace the progress of the speaker's feelings from the first line to the last. In this respect, pay special attention to the change in language and in the focus of the images.

    How do you interpret the title? What gives the poem its compressed power?

From the time of Plato's *Symposium,* which celebrates the bonds of art and friendship among men, poets have returned to this theme: friends separated by distance, poets speaking across time to each other, a teacher mourning the death of a student, a son in the tearing sorrow of his father's death.

Exile's Letter

Rihaku

Translated by Ezra Pound

To So-Kin of Rakuyo, ancient friend, Chancellor of
    Gen.
Now I remember that you built me a special tavern
By the south side of the bridge at Ten-Shin.
With yellow gold and white jewels, we paid for songs
    and laughter
And we were drunk for month on month, forgetting
    the kings and princes.   5
Intelligent men came drifting in from the sea and
    from the west border,
And with them, and with you especially
There was nothing at cross purpose,
And they made nothing of sea-crossing or of moun-
    tain-crossing,
If only they could be of that fellowship,   10
And we all spoke out our hearts and minds, and
    without regret.
And when I was sent off to South Wei,
        smothered in laurel groves,
And you to the north of Raku-hoku,

Rihaku: *Japanese name for the famous eighth-century Chinese poet Li Po. In this poem, in the form of a letter, he recalls some of the youthful pleasures he shared with an old friend.*

Till we had nothing but thoughts and memories in
    common.   15
And then, when separation had come to its worst,
We met, and travelled into Sen-Go,
Through all the thirty-six folds of the turning and
    twisting waters,
Into a valley of the thousand bright flowers,
That was the first valley;   20
And into ten thousand valleys full of voices and pine-
    winds.
And with silver harness and reins of gold,
Out came the East of Kan foreman and his company.
And there came also the "True man" of Shi-yo to
    meet me,
Playing on a jewelled mouth-organ.   25
In the storied houses of San-Ko they gave us more
    Sennin music,
Many instruments, like the sound of young phœnix
    broods.
The foreman of Kan Chu, drunk, danced
        because his long sleeves wouldn't keep still
With that music playing,   30
And I, wrapped in brocade, went to sleep with my
    head on his lap,
And my spirit so high it was all over the heavens,
And before the end of the day we were scattered like
    stars, or rain.
I had to be off to So, far away over the waters,
You back to your river-bridge.   35

And your father, who was brave as a leopard,
Was governor in Hei Shu, and put down the bar-
    barian rabble.
And one May he had you send for me,
        despite the long distance.
And what with broken wheels and so on, I won't say

it wasn't hard going,   40
Over roads twisted like sheep's guts.
And I was still going, late in the year,
       in the cutting wind from the North,
And thinking how little you cared for the cost,
       and you caring enough to pay it.   45
And what a reception:
Red jade cups, food well set on a blue jewelled table,
And I was drunk, and had no thought of returning.
And you would walk out with me to the western
       corner of the castle,
To the dynastic temple, with water about it clear as
       blue jade,   50
With boats floating, and the sound of mouth-organs
       and drums,
With ripples like dragon-scales, going grass green on
       the water,
Pleasure lasting, with courtezans, going and coming
       without hindrance,
With the willow flakes falling like snow,
And the vermilioned girls getting drunk about sunset,   55
And the water, a hundred feet deep, reflecting green
       eyebrows
— Eyebrows painted green are a fine sight in young
       moonlight,
Gracefully painted —
And the girls singing back at each other,
Dancing in transparent brocade,   60
And the wind lifting the song, and interrupting it,
Tossing it up under the clouds.
              And all this comes to an end.
              And is not again to be met with.
I went up to the court for examination,   65
Tried Layu's luck, offered the Choyo song,
And got no promotion,
              and went back to the East Mountains

White-headed.
And once again, later, we met at the South bridge-
    head.   70
And then the crowd broke up, you went north to San
    palace,
And if you ask how I regret that parting:
It is like the flowers falling at Spring's end
        Confused, whirled in a tangle.
What is the use of talking, and there is no end of
    talking,   75
There is no end of things in the heart.
I call in the boy,
Have him sit on his knees here
        To seal this,
And send it a thousand miles, thinking.   80

As I Step Over a Puddle at the End of Winter, I Think of an Ancient Chinese Governor

James Wright

> *And how can I, born in evil days*
> *And fresh from failure, ask a kindness*
> *of Fate?*
> — Written A.D. 819

Po Chu-i,* balding old politician,
What's the use?
I think of you,
Uneasily entering the gorges of the Yang-Tze,
When you were being towed up the rapids   5
Toward some political job or other

1. Po Chu-i: *a statesman of the T'ang dynasty (618–906 B.C.) and also a great classical poet.*

In the city of Chungshou.
You made it, I guess,
By dark.

But it is 1960, it is almost spring again,   10
And the tall rocks of Minneapolis
Build me my own black twilight
Of bamboo ropes and waters.
Where is Yuan Chen, the friend you loved?
Where is the sea, that once solved the whole loneliness   15
Of the Midwest? Where is Minneapolis? I can see
    nothing
But the great terrible oak tree darkening with winter.
Did you find the city of isolated men beyond moun-
    tains?
Or have you been holding the end of a frayed rope
For a thousand years?
                                                                  20

A Supermarket in California

Allen Ginsberg

What thoughts I had of you tonight, Walt Whitman,
for I walked down the sidestreets under the trees with
a headache self-conscious looking at the full moon.

In my hungry fatigue, and shopping for images, I
went into the neon fruit supermarket, dreaming of   5
your enumerations!

What peaches and what penumbras! Whole families shopping at night! Aisles full of husbands!
Wives in the avocados, babies in the tomatoes! —
and you, García Lorca,* what were you doing down   10
by the watermelons?

10. García Lorca: *Spanish poet and playwright, whose career was prema-
turely ended by his murder at the hands of General Franco's followers during
the Spanish civil war. His "Somnambulistic Ballad" appears on page 168.*

I saw you, Walt Whitman, childless, lonely old grubber, poking among the meats in the refrigerator and eyeing the grocery boys.

I heard you asking questions of each: Who killed   15
the pork chops? What price bananas? Are you my Angel?

I wandered in and out of the brilliant stacks of cans following you, and followed in my imagination by the store detective.   20

We strode down the open corridors together in our solitary fancy tasting artichokes, possessing every frozen delicacy, and never passing the cashier.

Where are we going, Walt Whitman? The doors close in an hour. Which way does your beard point   25
tonight?

(I touch your book and dream of our odyssey in the supermarket and feel absurd.)

Will we walk all night through solitary streets? The trees add shade to shade, lights out in the houses,   30
we'll both be lonely.

Will we stroll dreaming of the lost America of love past blue automobiles in driveways, home to our silent cottage?

Ah, dear father, graybeard, lonely old courage-   35
teacher, what America did you have when Charon*
quit poling his ferry and you got out on a smoking bank and stood watching the boat disappear on the black waters of Lethe?*

---

36. Charon: *in classical mythology, the ferryman who conveyed the souls of the dead across the river to the gate of Hades.*
39. Lethe: *a mythological river, one of those separating Hades from the world above, whose water caused those who drank of it to forget everything of the past.*

In Memory of W. B. Yeats

(d. Jan. 1939)

W. H. Auden

1

He disappeared in the dead of winter:
The brooks were frozen, the airports almost deserted,
And snow disfigured the public statues;
The mercury sank in the mouth of the dying day.
O all the instruments agree   5
The day of his death was a dark cold day.

Far from his illness
The wolves ran on through the evergreen forests,
The peasant river was untempted by the fashionable
      quays;
By mourning tongues   10
The death of the poet was kept from his poems.

But for him it was his last afternoon as himself,
An afternoon of nurses and rumours;
The provinces of his body revolted,
The squares of his mind were empty,   15
Silence invaded the suburbs,
The current of his feeling failed: he became his
      admirers.

Now he is scattered among a hundred cities
And wholly given over to unfamiliar affections;
To find his happiness in another kind of wood   20
And be punished under a foreign code of conscience.
The words of a dead man
Are modified in the guts of the living.

But in the importance and noise of tomorrow

When the brokers are roaring like beasts on the floor
    of the Bourse,*　　25
And the poor have the sufferings to which they are
    fairly accustomed,
And each in the cell of himself is almost convinced of
    his freedom;
A few thousand will think of this day
As one thinks of a day when one did something
    slightly unusual.
O all the instruments agree　　30
The day of his death was a dark cold day.

2

You were silly like us: your gift survived it all;
The parish of rich women, physical decay,
Yourself; mad Ireland hurt you into poetry.
Now Ireland has her madness and her weather still,　　35
For poetry makes nothing happen: it survives
In the valley of its saying where executives
Would never want to tamper; it flows south
From ranches of isolation and the busy griefs,
Raw towns that we believe and die in; it survives,　　40
A way of happening, a mouth.

3

    Earth, receive an honoured guest;
    William Yeats is laid to rest:
    Let the Irish vessel lie
    Emptied of its poetry.　　45

    Time that is intolerant
    Of the brave and innocent,
    And indifferent in a week
    To a beautiful physique,

25. Bourse: *French stock exchange.*

Worships language and forgives   50
Everyone by whom it lives;
Pardons cowardice, conceit,
Lays its honours at their feet.

Time that with this strange excuse
Pardoned Kipling and his views,*   55
And will pardon Paul Claudel,*
Pardons him for writing well.

In the nightmare of the dark
All the dogs of Europe bark,
And the living nations wait,   60
Each sequestered in its hate;

Intellectual disgrace
Stares from every human face,
And the seas of pity lie
Locked and frozen in each eye.   65

Follow, poet, follow right
To the bottom of the night,
With your unconstraining voice
Still persuade us to rejoice;

With the farming of a verse   70
Make a vineyard of the curse,
Sing of human unsuccess
In a rapture of distress;

In the deserts of the heart
Let the healing fountain start,   75
In the prison of his days
Teach the free man how to praise.

---

55. Kipling . . . views: *Rudyard Kipling, a British literary figure of the nineteenth and early twentieth centuries, glorified English imperialism.*
56. Paul Claudel: *French literary figure of the same period, a political con-
servative.*

1. "Exile's Letter" is a translation from the Chinese. Added to the usual difficulties of rendering equivalent sound and associations in another language, there is the problem of translating an ideographic language such as Chinese into a symbolic one.

    How does Pound bridge the gap of many centuries and make the distant Chinese civilization seem authentic and close?

2. What parallels does James Wright (page 90) find between the world of Po Chu-i and his own, as expressed in the images of the poem? The last three lines suggest the kinship this modern poet feels for the Chinese poet-statesman. What is its basis?

3. What qualities does Ginsberg admire in Whitman, the man and the poet? How are they brought out by the form and the allusions of "A Supermarket in California" (page 92)? What is the significance of "Where are we going, Walt Whitman" (line 24)?

4. What qualities does Auden (page 94) admire in Yeats? In the third section of the poem, does Auden honor more Yeats's poetry or the role of the poet? What has Auden to say about poetry as a force for social regeneration?

    Why do you think Auden divided this poem into three disparate sections? What unites them, besides the subject?

5. Compare the language and tone of the last two poems with that of James Wright's poem. What different qualities emerge through the associations of the language used?

"After great pain a formal feeling comes," Emily Dickinson wrote, and elegies have traditionally been written with considerable formality. The structured words, like ritual, lend support when people need it most. In the second of the following elegies, Dylan Thomas uses an intricate form, the villanelle, with powerful originality; in Theodore Roethke's "Elegy for Jane," words and rhythms find their own natural, or organic, form.

Elegy for Jane

My Student, Thrown by a Horse

Theodore Roethke

I remember the neckcurls, limp and damp as tendrils;
And her quick look, a sidelong pickerel smile;
And how, once startled into talk, the light syllables
leaped for her,
And she balanced in the delight of her thought,
A wren, happy, tail into the wind,   5
Her song trembling the twigs and small branches.
The shade sang with her;
The leaves, their whispers turning to kissing;
And the mold sang in the bleached valleys under the
rose.

Oh, when she was sad, she cast herself down into
such a pure depth,   10
Even a father could not find her:
Scraping her cheek against straw;
Stirring the clearest water.

My sparrow, you are not here,
Waiting like a fern, making a spiny shadow.   15
The sides of wet stones cannot console me,
Nor the moss, wound with the last light.

If only I could nudge you from this sleep,
My maimed darling, my skittery pigeon.
Over this damp grave I speak the words of my love: 20
I, with no rights in this matter,
Neither father nor lover.

Do Not Go Gentle into That Good Night

Dylan Thomas

Do not go gentle into that good night,
Old age should burn and rave at close of day;
Rage, rage against the dying of the light.

Though wise men at their end know dark is right,
Because their words had forked no lightning they   5
Do not go gentle into that good night.

Good men, the last wave by, crying how bright
Their frail deeds might have danced in a green bay,
Rage, rage against the dying of the light.

Wild men who caught and sang the sun in flight,   10
And learn, too late, they grieved it on its way,
Do not go gentle into that good night.

Grave men, near death, who see with blinding sight
Blind eyes could blaze like meteors and be gay,
Rage, rage against the dying of the light.   15

And you, my father, there on the sad height,
Curse, bless, me now with your fierce tears, I pray.
Do not go gentle into that good night.
Rage, rage against the dying of the light.

1. Contrast the rhythmic patterns and sounds of these two poems.
   How do they support the development of mood in each? Read
   the poems aloud. What is striking in the way each poet uses language?

2. Show how the images in each of these elegies grow out of a single,
   central image, like a germinating seed — for instance, in Thomas's
   poem, "night/light."

3. What brings each of these poems to rest at the end? Contrast the
   effect of the endings.

The most selfless love of all, perhaps the only selfless love, gives to those who, being least lovable, need love most: the poor, the crippled in body or mind, the derelicts and outcasts of modern society.

The Hunchback in the Park

Dylan Thomas

The hunchback in the park
A solitary mister
Propped between trees and water
From the opening of the garden lock
That lets the trees and water enter   5
Until the Sunday sombre bell at dark

Eating bread from a newspaper
Drinking water from the chained cup
That the children filled with gravel
In the fountain basin where I sailed my ship   10
Slept at night in a dog kennel
But nobody chained him up.

Like the park birds he came early
Like the water he sat down
And Mister they called Hey mister   15
The truant boys from the town
Running when he had heard them clearly
On out of sound

Past lake and rockery
Laughing when he shook his paper   20
Hunchbacked in mockery
Through the loud zoo of the willow groves

Dodging the park keeper
With his stick that picked up leaves.

And the old dog sleeper   25
Alone between nurses and swans
While the boys among willows
Made the tigers jump out of their eyes
To roar on the rockery stones
And the groves were blue with sailors   30

Made all day until bell time
A woman figure without fault
Straight as a young elm
Straight and tall from his crooked bones
That she might stand in the night   35
After the locks and chains

All night in the unmade park
After the railings and shrubberies
The birds the grass the trees the lake
And the wild boys innocent as strawberries   40
Had followed the hunchback
To his kennel in the dark.

Stumpfoot on 42nd Street

Louis Simpson

A Negro sprouts from the pavement like an asparagus.
One hand beats a drum and cymbal;
He plays a trumpet with the other.

He flies the American flag;
When he goes walking, from stump to stump.   5
It twitches, and swoops, and flaps.

Also, he has a tin cup which he rattles;
He shoves it right in your face.
These freaks are alive in earnest.

He is not embarrassed.   10
It is for you to feel embarrassed,
Or God, or the way things are.

Therefore he plays the trumpet
And therefore he beats the drum.

2

I can see myself in Venezuela,   15
With flowers, and clouds in the distance.
The mind tends to drift.

But Stumpfoot stands near a window
Advertising cameras, trusses, household utensils.
The billboards twinkle. The time   20
Is 12:26.

O why don't angels speak in the infinite
To each other? Why this confusion,
These particular bodies —
Eros with clenched fists, sobbing and cursing?   25

The time is 12:26.
The streets lead on in burning lines
And giants tremble in electric chains.

3

I can see myself in the middle of Venezuela
Stepping in a nest of ants.   30
I can see myself being eaten by ants.

My ribs are caught in a thorn bush
And thought has no reality.
But he has furnished his room

With a chair and table.   35
A chair is like a dog, it waits for man.
He unstraps his apparatus,

And now he is taking off his boots.
He is easing his stumps,
And now he is lighting a cigar.   40

It seems that a man exists
Only to say, Here I am in person.

The Child Next Door

Robert Penn Warren

The child next door is defective because the mother,
Seven brats already in that purlieu* of dirt,
Took a pill, or did something to herself she thought
     would not hurt,
But it did, and no good, for there came this monstrous
     other.

The sister is twelve. Is beautiful like a saint.   5
Sits with the monster all day, with pure love, calm
     eyes.
Has taught it a trick, to make *ciao*,* Italian-wise.
It crooks hand in that greeting. She smiles her smile
     without taint.

2. purlieu: *surroundings, atmosphere.*
7. *ciao: pronounced "chow," an Italian greeting.*

I come, and her triptych* beauty and joy stir hate
— Is it hate? — in my heart. Fool, doesn't she know
    that the process   10
Is not that joyous or simple, to bless, or unbless,
The malfeasance* of nature or the filth of fate?

Can it bind or loose,* that beauty in that kind,
Beauty of benediction? I trust our hope to prevail
That heart-joy in beauty be wisdom, before beauty
    fail   15
And be gathered like air in the ruck of the world's
    wind!

I think of your goldness, of joy, how empires grind,
    stars are hurled.
I smile stiff, saying *ciao*, saying *ciao*, and think: this is
    the world.

9. triptych: *three-paneled picture, often an altarpiece. The sister is thus compared to a painted figure of saintly beauty.*
12. malfeasance: *bad conduct.*
13. bind or loose: *reference to the power conferred by Christ upon Peter.*

Complaint

William Carlos Williams

They call me and I go.
It is a frozen road
past midnight, a dust
of snow caught
in the rigid wheeltracks.   5
The door opens.
I smile, enter and
shake off the cold.

Here is a great woman
on her side in the bed.   10
She is sick,
perhaps vomiting,
perhaps laboring
to give birth to
a tenth child. Joy! Joy!   15

Night is a room
darkened for lovers,
through the jalousies the sun
has sent one gold needle!
I pick the hair from her eyes   20
and watch her misery
with compassion.

1. The last four poems all persuade us to compassion. How deeply
   is the speaker involved in each case? Which poem do you think
   succeeds best in expressing the modern feeling about suffering?
   Why?

2. What questions do "Stumpfoot" and "The Child Next Door" ask,
   directly or indirectly? Are the questions answered? Can you state
   the argument of "The Child Next Door," stanza by stanza?

4

My Townspeople

People are endlessly interesting to people, and the experience of knowing different people has never been more varied than today, when, to take a single example, people living in a stone-age world are seen on television by others living in a science-fiction time — and vice versa.

People watch each other idly gathered at a bus stop or demonstrating in the street; they read "Dear Abby" letters in the newspaper and steal candid shots of each other in strange cities. The popularization of modern psychology has made people more curious about the peculiar behavior of others. Still, man remains a mystery to man: complex and unpredictable and still evolving.

However, long before the science of psychology, poets penetrated men's masks to the real self behind them. Working intuitively, the poet recreates people through images drawn from his own rich memory and in language mined from his own experience. He shows us what it is like to be alive at a particular crossroad in time/space.

The poet Archibald MacLeish wrote, "It is when the human heart faces its destiny and notwithstanding sings — sings of itself, its life, its death — that poetry is possible."

The poet takes the degradations, the misery, the cruel and senseless human experiences, and shows that man transcends these.

These first two poems present very different worlds. How simple and certain is the old man's world in Merwin's poem — a world now past, smaller in possibilities than ours, but safer. Robert Lowell's "Skunk Hour," in contrast, evokes the fragmented and confused modern world: the predicament of the lost self is a recurrent twentieth-century theme.

Grandfather in the Old Men's Home

W. S. Merwin

Gentle, at last, and as clean as ever,
He did not even need drink any more,
And his good sons unbent and brought him
Tobacco to chew, both times when they came
To be satisfied he was well cared for.   5
And he smiled all the time to remember
Grandmother, his wife, wearing the true faith
Like an iron nightgown, yet brought to birth
Seven times and raising the family
Through her needle's eye while he got away   10
Down the green river, finding directions
For boats. And himself coming home sometimes
Well-heeled but blind drunk, to hide all the bread
And shoot holes in the bucket while he made
His daughters pump. Still smiled as kindly in   15
His sleep beside the other clean old men
To see Grandmother, every night the same,
Huge in her age, with her thumbed-down mouth, come
Hating the river, filling with her stare
His gliding dream, while he turned to water,   20

While the children they both had begotten,
With old faces now, but themselves shrunken
To child-size again, stood ranged at her side,
Beating their little Bibles till he died.

Skunk Hour

For Elizabeth Bishop

Robert Lowell

Nautilus Island's hermit
heiress still lives through winter in her Spartan
    cottage;
her sheep still graze above the sea.
Her son's a bishop. Her farmer
is first selectman in our village;   5
she's in her dotage.

Thirsting for
the hierarchic privacy
of Queen Victoria's century,
she buys up all
the eyesores facing her shore,   10
and lets them fall.

The season's ill —
we've lost our summer millionaire,
who seemed to leap from an L. L. Bean
catalogue. His nine-knot yawl   15
was auctioned off to lobstermen.
A red fox stain covers Blue Hill.

And now our fairy
decorator brightens his shop for fall;   20

his fishnet's filled with orange cork,
orange, his cobbler's bench and awl;
there is no money in his work,
he'd rather marry.

One dark night,   25
my Tudor Ford climbed the hill's skull;
I watched for love-cars. Lights turned down,
they lay together, hull to hull,
where the graveyard shelves on the town. . . .
My mind's not right.   30

A car radio bleats,
"Love, O careless Love. . . ." I hear
my ill-spirit sob in each blood cell,
as if my hand were at its throat. . . .
I myself am hell;   35
nobody's here —

only skunks, that search
in the moonlight for a bite to eat.
They march on their soles up Main Street:
white stripes, moonstruck eyes' red fire   40
under the chalk-dry and spar spire
of the Trinitarian Church.

I stand on top
of our back steps and breathe the rich air —
a mother skunk with her column of kittens swills the
        garbage pail.   45
She jabs her wedge-head in a cup
of sour cream, drops her ostrich tail,
and will not scare.

1. What are the relationships between the grandfather and the members of his family in the Merwin poem? With what ironic touches

does the poet show the family? What meanings are developed for the water symbol in this poem?

2. Robert Lowell wrote, "Meaning is only a strand and an element in the brute flow of composition. Other elements are pictures that please or thrill for themselves, phrases that ring for their music or carry some buried suggestions. For all this the author is an opportunist, throwing whatever comes to hand into his feeling for start, continuity, contrast, climax and completion." Can you refer any of the elements Lowell mentions to "Skunk Hour"?

3. Are the images of Lowell's poem as random as they seem, or is there some quality they share that gives them coherence?

One of the themes of "Skunk Hour" is that the times are out of joint. When that is so, it is the young who suffer most. No class or race is immune, as the next poems witness.

Junior Addict

Langston Hughes

The little boy
who sticks a needle in his arm
and seeks an out in other worldly dreams,
who seeks an out in eyes that droop
and ears that close to Harlem screams,   5
cannot know, of course,
(and has no way to understand)
a sunrise that he cannot see
beginning in some other land —
but destined sure to flood — and soon —   10

the very room in which he leaves
his needle and his spoon,
the very room in which today the air
is heavy with the drug
of his despair.   15

    (Yet little can
    tomorrow's sunshine give
    to one who will not live.)

Quick, sunrise, come —
Before the mushroom bomb   20
Pollutes his stinking air
With better death
Than is his living here,
With viler drugs
Than bring today's release   25
In poison from the fallout
Of our peace.

    "It's easier to get dope
    than it is to get a job."

Yes, easier to get dope   30
than to get a job —
daytime or nightime job,
teen-age, pre-draft,
pre-lifetime job.

Quick, sunrise, come!   35
Sunrise out of Africa,
Quick, come!
Sunrise, please come!
Come! Come!

We Real Cool

The Pool Players.
Seven at the Golden Shovel.

Gwendolyn Brooks

We real cool. We
Left school. We

Lurk late. We
Strike straight. We

Sing sin. We   5
Thin gin. We

Jazz June. We
Die soon.

Wild Orphan

Allen Ginsberg

Blandly mother
takes him strolling
    by railroad and by river
— he's the son of the absconded
    hot rod angel —   5
and he imagines cars
    and rides them in his dreams,

so lonely growing up among
    the imaginary automobiles
and dead souls of Tarrytown   10

    to create
out of his own imagination
    the beauty of his wild
forebears — a mythology
    he cannot inherit.   15

Will he later hallucinate
    his gods? Waking
among mysteries with
    an insane gleam
of recollection?   20

    The recognition —
something so rare
    in his soul,
met only in dreams
    — nostalgias   25
of another life.

A question of the soul.
    And the injured

losing their injury
    in their innocence   30
— a cock, a cross,
    an excellence of love.

And the father grieves
    in flophouse
complexities of memory   35
    a thousand miles
away, unknowing
    of the unexpected
youthful stranger
    bumming toward his door.   40

The Youngest Schizophrene

Katherine Hoskins

Bite-lip brave and militant,
She clips Hello and settles daunt-
less to her own — O, catch as catch
Once could — her kin; uneasy watch
    That she must stand each week.   5

And bluffest old campaigners, we
Make room beside the fire, we
Kind talk provide and family bruit
To jolly up the young recruit.
    But to her fear-taut, ghost-   10

Corrupted face, we cannot brag
Of certain magic, unseamed rags
We diced for; nor not confess that

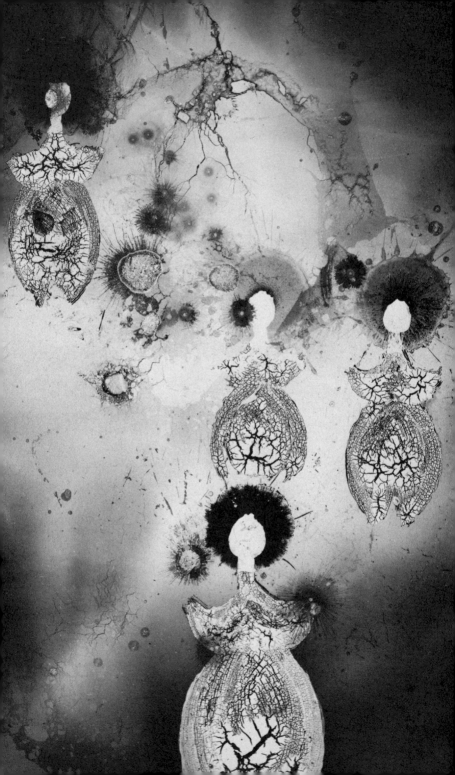

We won but briefest bivouac
    On wintry Golgotha;*   15

That gambling for the garment, we
The Life left rotting on a tree.

Words lapse, the fire dies.
Not hers but Christ's own tiger eyes
    Accuse us from the dark.   20

15. Golgotha: *the hill of Calvary, where Christ was
crucified by Roman soldiers, who afterward gambled
for his unseamed cloak.*

1. The preceding four poems are all written by adults about children.
How far are they able to suggest the reality of the young person's
experience, which they see only from the outside? In this regard,
consider the amount of insight (not just sympathy) shown and the
tone of the speaker.

2. Notice how unusual the language is in "The Youngest Schizophrene" — how dense it is, how congruous with image and sound
impressions.

What analogy between the present and the past is established by
the allusions to the army and the crucifixion?

The twentieth century has seen a record amount of mental illness. Those who come back find it impossible to describe; those who have never been there see only the baffling surface. The next poem suggests some of the reality of that other world. Notice how the poet turns each image to imagelessness, creating substance out of the reiteration of empty words.

Madhouse

Calvin C. Hernton

Here is a place that is no place
And here is no place that is a place
A place somewhere beyond the reaches of time
And beyond the reaches of those who in time
Bring flowers and fruit to this place,   5
Yet here is a definite place
And a definite time, fixed
In a timelessness of precise vantage
From which to view flowers and view fruit
And those who come bearing them.   10

Those who come by Sunday's habit are weary
And kiss us half-foreign but sympathetic,
Spread and eat noisily to crack the unbearable
Silence of this place:
They do not know that something must always come   15
From something and that nothing must come always
From nothing, and that nothing is always a thing

To drive us mad.

Underlying these severe problems is a general and growing sense of alienation among men, of individual isolation even in the midst of crowded places:

Brooding

David Ignatow

The sadness of our lives.
We will never be good enough to each other,
to our parents and friends.
We go along like old sailing ships,
loaded with food and drink for a long voyage,   5
self-sufficient, without any outside contact
with the world.
                    The truth faces me
all the time. We are in a world
in which nobody listens to anybody,   10
in which we do as we please
until we are stopped by others.
We live our whole lives as in a husk,
which keeps us separate from any influence.
While those who reflect the influence   15
of others are either idiots, or people
who never gained consciousness.

1. How true is it in your experience that "nobody listens to anybody" and that "we do as we please / until we are stopped by others"?

2. What is the tone of the last three lines of the poem? Are they to be taken at face value?

There are also those who stand outside society altogether: the scapegoats, the awakening minorities, the dispossessed. Some move through the world without being seen, their very existence denied. Others live with a burden of guilt.

Saint Judas

James Wright

When I went out to kill myself,* I caught
A pack of hoodlums beating up a man.
Running to spare his suffering, I forgot
My name, my number, how my day began,
How soldiers milled around the garden stone   5
And sang amusing songs; how all that day
Their javelins measured crowds; how I alone
Bargained the proper coins, and slipped away.

Banished from heaven, I found this victim beaten,
Stripped, kneed, and left to cry. Dropping my rope   10
Aside, I ran, ignored the uniforms:
Then I remembered bread my flesh had eaten,*
The kiss that ate my flesh.* Flayed without hope,
I held the man for nothing in my arms.

1. When I . . . myself: *According to the Gospel of Matthew, Judas Iscariot, after betraying Christ to his enemies for thirty pieces of silver, returned the money and hanged himself.*
12. bread . . . eaten: *Shortly before the betrayal, Judas had been present at the Last Supper, when Christ gave the disciples bread to eat from his hands, telling them it was his flesh, which was to be broken like the bread.*
13. kiss . . . flesh: *A kiss was Judas's means of identifying Christ to the soldiers who came to arrest him.*

My Great-Grandfather's Slaves

Wendell Berry

Deep in the back ways of my mind I see them
    going in the long days
    over the same fields that I have gone
    long days over.

I see the sun passing and burning high   5
    over that land from their day
    until mine, their shadows
    having risen and consumed them.

I see them obeying and watching
    the bearded tall man whose voice   10
    and blood are mine, whose countenance

in stone at his grave my own resembles,
    whose blindness is my brand.

I see them kneel and pray to the white God
    who buys their souls with Heaven.   15

I see them approach, quiet
    in the merchandise of their flesh,
    to put down their burdens
    of firewood and hemp and tobacco
    into the minds of my kinsmen.   20

I see them moving in the rooms of my history,
    the day of my birth entering
    the horizon emptied of their days,
    their purchased lives taken back
    into the dust of birthright.   25

I see them borne, shadow within shadow,
    shroud within shroud, through all nights
    from their lives to mine, long beyond
    reparation or given liberty
    or any straightness.   30

I see them go in the bonds of my blood
    through all the time of their bodies.

I have seen that freedom cannot be taken
    from one man and given to another,
    and cannot be taken and kept.   35

I know that freedom can only be given,
    and is the gift to the giver
    from the one who receives.

I am owned by the blood of all of them
    who ever were owned by my blood.   40
    We cannot be free of each other.

The Concealment: Ishi, the Last Wild Indian

William Stafford

A rock, a leaf, mud, even the grass
Ishi the shadow man had to put back where it was.
In order to live he had to hide that he did.
His deep canyon he kept unmarked for the world,
and only his face became lined, because no one saw it   5
and it therefore didn't make any difference.

If he appeared, he died; and he was the last. Erased
footprints, berries that purify the breath, rituals
before dawn with water — even the dogs roamed a
        land
unspoiled by Ishi, who used to own it, with his aunt   10
and uncle, whose old limbs bound in willow bark
        finally
stopped and were hidden under the rocks, in sweet
        leaves.

We ought to help change that kind of premature
        suicide,
the existence gradually mottled away till the heartbeat
blends and the messages all go one way from the
        world   15
and disappear inward: Ishi lived. It was all right
for him to make a track. In California now where his
        opposites
unmistakably dwell we wander their streets

And sometimes whisper his name —
"Ishi."   20

Ishi, starving and desperate, stumbled into a California town in the summer of 1911. He was literally a stone-age man, the last of a tribe. The story of his survival in the woods and his adjustment to twentieth-century civilization is told in Ishi: In Two Worlds, *by Theodora Kroeber, University of California Press, 1961.*

1. Besides being an account of an individual life, each of the preceding poems can be seen as a metaphor of man's journey here
   on earth. How are they each developed to suggest a bigger scheme
   of things?

2. What is the paradox of "Saint Judas"? How does Wright's short
   drama differ from the traditional story of Judas's life?

3. How do the form and the images in "My Great-Grandfather's
   Slaves" combine to advance and expand the urgency of the poem?

   What changes in phrasing and rhythm strengthen the turn to
   abstract statements in the last part of the poem?

Luckily, some people are free and fortunate, their lives whole and
fulfilling. As artists, scientists, they walk the heights, pushing toward
the new and unimagined. Man, they remind us, is a maker, ex-
hilarated by the order and consistency he can bring out of the
confusion of experience.

Sext

W. H. Auden

You need not see what someone is doing
to know if it is his vocation,

Sext: *fourth of the seven daily prayer times in Catholic churches. This is the
first section of a poem on the theme that civilization and guilt have gone hand
in hand as man rose above the level of the animals. Nevertheless the poet
praises life as joyous, although inescapably sinful.*

you have only to watch his eyes:
a cook mixing a sauce, a surgeon

making a primary incision,   5
a clerk completing a bill of lading,

wear the same rapt expression,
forgetting themselves in a function.

How beautiful it is,
that eye-on-the-object look.   10

To ignore the appetitive goddesses,
to desert the formidable shrines

of Rhea, Aphrodite, Demeter, Diana,
to pray instead to St. Phocas,

St. Barbara, San Saturnino,   15
or whoever one's patron is,

that one may be worthy of their mystery,
what a prodigious step to have taken.

There should be monuments, there should be odes,
to the nameless heroes who took it first,   20

to the first flaker of flints
who forgot his dinner,

the first collector of sea-shells
to remain celibate.

Where should we be but for them?   25
Feral still, un-housetrained, still

wandering through forests without
a consonant to our names,

slaves of Dame Kind, lacking
all notion of a city,   30

and, at this noon, for this death,*
there would be no agents.

31. this death: *the crucifixion of Christ, as it stands*
for the guilt of all men.

Musée des Beaux Arts

W. H. Auden

About suffering they were never wrong,
The Old Masters: how well they understood
Its human position; how it takes place
While someone else is eating or opening a window or
        just walking dully along;
How, when the aged are reverently, passionately
        waiting   5
For the miraculous birth, there always must be
Children who did not specially want it to happen,
        skating
On a pond at the edge of the wood:

They never forgot
That even the dreadful martyrdom must run its course   10
Anyhow in a corner, some untidy spot
Where the dogs go on with their doggy life and the
        torturer's horse
Scratches its innocent behind on a tree.

In Brueghel's *Icarus*,* for instance: how everything
    turns away
Quite leisurely from the disaster; the ploughman may   15
Have heard the splash, the forsaken cry,
But for him it was not an important failure; the sun
    shone
As it had to on the white legs disappearing into the
    green
Water; and the expensive delicate ship that must have
    seen
Something amazing, a boy falling out of the sky,   20
Had somewhere to get to and sailed calmly on.

14. Brueghel's *Icarus:* The Fall of Icarus, *a painting by Pieter Brueghel, a sixteenth-century Flemish painter. According to Greek mythology, Icarus, wearing a pair of wings made by his father, flew too near the sun. The wax of his wings melted, and he fell into the sea.*

Peter Quince at the Clavier

Wallace Stevens

I

Just as my fingers on these keys
Make music, so the selfsame sounds
On my spirit make a music, too.

Music is feeling, then, not sound;
And thus it is that what I feel,   5
Here in this room, desiring you,

Clavier: *early keyboard instrument.*

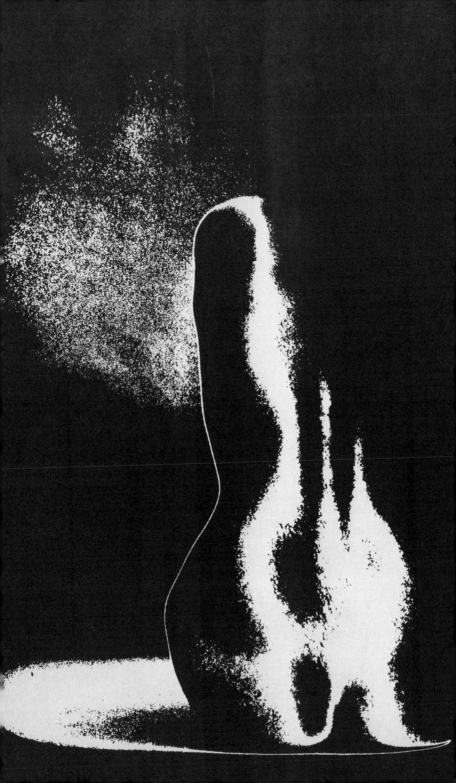

Thinking of your blue-shadowed silk,
Is music. It is like the strain
Waked in the elders by Susanna.*

Of a green evening, clear and warm,   10
She bathed in her still garden, while
The red-eyed elders watching, felt

The basses of their beings throb
In witching chords, and their thin blood
Pulse pizzicati* of Hosanna.*   15

        II

In the green water, clear and warm,
Susanna lay.
She searched
The touch of springs,
And found   20
Concealed imaginings.
She sighed,
For so much melody.

Upon the bank, she stood
In the cool   25
Of spent emotions
She felt, among the leaves,
The dew
Of old devotions.

---

9. elders . . . Susanna: *One of the books of the Old Testament Apocrypha tells how Susanna was accused of adultery by certain Jewish elders who, during her husband's absence, unsuccessfully tried to seduce her.*
15. pizzicati: *notes played on a string instrument by plucking the strings with the fingers instead of the bow.* Hosanna: *a cry of praise or adoration.*

She walked upon the grass,   30
Still quavering.
The winds were like her maids,
On timid feet,
Fetching her woven scarves,
Yet wavering.   35

A breath upon her hand
Muted the night.
She turned —
A cymbal crashed,
And roaring horns.   40

III

Soon, with a noise like tambourines,
Came her attendant Byzantines.

They wondered why Susanna cried
Against the elders by her side;

And as they whispered, the refrain   45
Was like a willow swept by rain.

Anon, their lamps' uplifted flame
Revealed Susanna and her shame.

And then, the simpering Byzantines
Fled, with a noise like tambourines.   50

IV

Beauty is momentary in the mind —
The fitful tracing of a portal;
But in the flesh it is immortal.

The body dies; the body's beauty lives.
So evenings die, in their green going,   55

A wave, interminably flowing.
So gardens die, their meek breath scenting
The cowl of winter, done repenting.
So maidens die, to the auroral
Celebration of a maiden's choral.   60

Susanna's music touched the bawdy strings
Of those white elders; but, escaping,
Left only Death's ironic scraping.
Now, in its immortality, it plays
On the clear viol of her memory,   65
And makes a constant sacrament of praise.

1. How does a poet incorporate philosophical ideas into his poetry?
    T. S. Eliot wrote that "the poet who 'thinks' is merely the poet who
    can express the emotional equivalent of thought"; that it is not the
    function of the poet to be an original thinker, but rather to make his
    poetry out of the thinking of his age. Consider these statements in
    relation to the preceding poems. How are emotion-charged
    images — the "emotional equivalent of thought" — used to express
    ideas? At what point in these poems does the image become
    metaphor for an idea?

2. What connection has "Sext" with prayer? It seems at first a simple
    celebration of man's joy in craftsmanship, but the last couplet
    brings us up short. Can you explain Auden's ambivalent attitude?

3. In "Musée des Beaux Arts" the first stanza alludes to other paint-
    ings of the Old Masters. What was it, according to Auden, that they
    understood about suffering? Does Auden imply that we understand
    less well today, or differently, or what? In this regard, read "The
    Hunchback in the Park" (page 102), "Stumpfoot on 42nd Street"
    (page 103), "The Child Next Door" (page 105), and "Complaint"
    (page 106). What images in these poems can be compared to the
    painted images of the Old Masters? What does the phrasing of the
    different poems suggest about the modern conception, or miscon-
    ception, of suffering and of people's attitude toward it?

4. One of the major themes in Wallace Stevens's poetry is man as
    the maker of reality. Trace, in the four movements of "Peter
    Quince," the variety of ways in which Stevens develops this theme.
    Compare the four movements in their new fusion of melodic, intel-
    lectual, and visual elements.

Wallace Stevens wrote that the poet's "function is to make his imagination become the light in the minds of others. His role . . . is to help people live their lives." He is "the intermediary between people and the world in which they live, and also between people as between themselves."

Stevens cannot mean this in a literal way — a poet is neither a moralist nor a teacher. But in another way the poet does in fact "become the light in the minds of others" — by showing people wider ways of being and of acting and of feeling than the experience of their own lives could provide. Imagination — imaging — is the key.

Tract

William Carlos Williams

I will teach you my townspeople
how to perform a funeral —
for you have it over a troop
of artists —
unless one should scour the world —   5
you have the ground sense necessary.

See! the hearse leads.
I begin with a design for a hearse.
For Christ's sake not black —
nor white either — and not polished!   10
Let it be weathered — like a farm wagon —
with gilt wheels (this could be
applied fresh at small expense)
or no wheels at all:
a rough dray to drag over the ground.   15

Knock the glass out!
My God — glass, my townspeople!
For what purpose? Is it for the dead

to look out or for us to see
how well he is housed or to see   20
the flowers or the lack of them —
or what?
To keep the rain and snow from him?
He will have a heavier rain soon:
pebbles and dirt and what not.   25
Let there be no glass —
and no upholstery phew!
and no little brass rollers
and small easy wheels on the bottom —
my townspeople what are you thinking of?   30

A rough plain hearse then
with gilt wheels and no top at all.
On this the coffin lies
by its own weight.

        No wreaths please —   35
especially no hot house flowers.
Some common memento is better,
something he prized and is known by:
his old clothes — a few books perhaps —
God knows what! You realize   40
how we are about these things
my townspeople —
something will be found — anything
even flowers if he had come to that.
So much for the hearse.   45

For heaven's sake though see to the driver!
Take off the silk hat! In fact
that's no place at all for him —
up there unceremoniously
dragging our friend out to his own dignity!   50
Bring him down — bring him down!
Low and inconspicuous! I'd not have him ride

on the wagon at all — damn him —
the undertaker's understrapper!
Let him hold the reins   55
and walk at the side
and inconspicuously too!

Then briefly as to yourselves:
Walk behind — as they do in France,
seventh class, or if you ride   60
Hell take curtains! Go with some show
of inconvenience; sit openly —
to the weather as to grief.
Or do you think you can shut grief in?
What — from us? We who have perhaps   65
nothing to lose? Share with us
share with us — it will be money
in your pockets.
                                        Go now
I think you are ready.   70

Yardbird's Skull

For Charlie Parker

Owen Dodson

The bird is lost,
Dead, with all the music:
Whole sunsets heard the brain's music
Faded to last horizon notes.
I do not know why I hold   5
This skull, smaller than a walnut's,
Against my ear,
Expecting to hear

Charlie Parker: *alto saxophonist and composer, one of America's
most important jazz musicians. He was thirty-five when he died.
Parker was nicknamed "Bird."*

The smashed fear
Of childhood from . . . bone;   10
Expecting to see
Wind nosing red and purple,
Strange gold and magic
On bubbled windowpanes
Of childhood. Shall I hear?   15
I should hear: this skull
Has been with violets
Not Yorick, or the gravedigger,
Yapping his yelling story,*
This skull has been in air,   20

18–19. Yorick . . . story: *Hamlet, in Shakespeare's play, finds a
skull identified by the joking gravedigger as belonging to Yorick, a
former court jester.*

Sensed his brother, the swallow,
(Its talent for snow and crumbs).
Flown to lost Atlantis islands,
Places of dreaming, swimming lemmings.*
O I shall hear skull skull,   25
Hear your lame music,
Believe music rejects undertaking,
Limps back.
Remember tiny lasting, we get lonely:
Come sing, come sing, come sing sing   30
And sing.

24. lemmings: *The mass migrations of these small rodents often lead them into the sea, where great numbers are drowned.*

5

The Box Is Locked

The conflict that most bitterly divides the mind of modern man against itself is the conflict between reason and instinct, between the objective world where science rules and the subjective reality of our inner life.

Poets lean to the side of instinct. For instance, to many people dreams and the life of the subconscious are only a brief and soon-forgotten puzzle. But poets have always taken their visions seriously, and from these strange and powerful and mysterious images they have created myths — myths we can never quite explain though we recognize their truth. Thus poetry, even the most rational, begins and ends in mystery. Its very ambiguity draws people back again and again for greater understanding.

Yet twentieth-century man, trained in the scientific method and conditioned to a matter-of-fact view of the world, usually mistrusts intuitions that have no rational explanation. Perhaps in reaction to this materialistic viewpoint, contemporary poetry has shown a strong impulse toward the irrational. This goes beyond the use of selected dream images as symbols — as, for example, in Yeats's "The Second Coming" (page 8) — beyond the conscious attempt to recreate an otherwise incommunicable experience, as Calvin Hernton does in "Madhouse." From the underworld of the subconscious the poet sets out to fish living things, visions which he must resist the impulse to rationalize. These are primal messages coded in sense symbols, and the poet must see them through, as undamaged as possible, into the word/music patterns of poetry. These visions are as real as they are strange; they bear fantastically authentic truths: the ancients believed they were cryptic messages from the gods. They seem to come to the poet, as Sylvia Plath suggests (page 161), in a locked box.

In times when common beliefs were shared by people through the medium of myths, the poet had only to touch on one of these sacred stories to release its stored emotion into the context of a new poem. Even today the old myths, recreated by modern poets, speak powerfully to our deepest intuitions.

Leda and the Swan

William Butler Yeats

A sudden blow: the great wings beating still
Above the staggering girl, her thighs caressed
By the dark webs, her nape caught in his bill,
He holds her helpless breast upon his breast.

How can those terrified vague fingers push   5
The feathered glory from her loosening thighs?
And how can body, laid in that white rush,
But feel the strange heart beating where it lies?

A shudder in the loins engenders there
The broken wall, the burning roof and tower   10
And Agamemnon dead.*
                     Being so caught up,
So mastered by the brute blood of the air,
Did she put on his knowledge with his power
Before the indifferent beak could let her drop?   15

"Leda and the Swan": *According to the Greek myth, Zeus visited Leda in the form of a swan. Their offspring was the famous Helen of Troy.*
11. Agamemnon dead: *Agamemnon, one of the Greek heroes of the Trojan war, was murdered by his wife when he returned home. (The cause of the war was the abduction of Leda's daughter Helen.)*

Bavarian Gentians

D. H. Lawrence

Not every man has gentians in his house
in Soft September, at slow, sad Michaelmas.

Bavarian gentians, big and dark, only dark
darkening the day-time, torch-like with the smoking
    blueness of Pluto's gloom,*
ribbed and torch-like, with their blaze of darkness
    spread blue   5
down flattening into points, flattened under the
    sweep of white day
torch-flower of the blue-smoking darkness, Pluto's
    dark-blue daze,
black lamps from the halls of Dis, burning dark blue,
giving off darkness, blue darkness, as Demeter's pale
    lamps* give off light,
lead me then, lead the way.   10

Reach me a gentian, give me a torch!
let me guide myself with the blue, forked torch of this
    flower
down the darker and darker stairs, where blue is
    darkened on blueness
even where Persephone goes, just now, from the
    frosted September
to the sightless realm where darkness is awake upon
    the dark   15

---

4. Pluto's gloom: *In Greek and Roman mythology Pluto (Dis) was the god of
the underworld.*
9. Demeter's . . . lamps: *Armed with torches, Demeter searched over the
world for her daughter Persephone, who had been abducted by Pluto. Angered
by Pluto's deed, Demeter allowed no vegetation to grow on earth. Finally it was
agreed that Persephone could spend four months of the year above ground,
during which time her mother allowed the earth to blossom (spring and summer).*

and Persephone herself is but a voice
or a darkness invisible enfolded in the deeper dark
of the arms Plutonic, and pierced with the passion of
    dense gloom,
among the splendour of torches of darkness, shedding
    darkness on the lost bride and her groom.

1. In Yeats's treatment of the Leda myth, the point of view is taken from deep inside Leda, her subjective feelings during the encounter. What is gained by this point of view? What is the "feathered glory" and "strange heart"?

2. What is the form of this poem? What purpose is served by the separate parts, and their relation to each other? What is the meaning of the sestet? What question does Yeats ask but refrain from answering?

3. "Leda" and "The Second Coming" (page 8) parallel each other in a way: each announces the advent of a new era in Western civilization. What does Yeats seem to have believed about the cycles of history? about man's relation to them?

4. When Lawrence wrote "Bavarian Gentians," he knew he was dying. How does he face death? What is the tone of the poem? What is the effect of colliding images like "blaze of darkness"? of the intense images of darkness carried along on the incantatory rhythm? What personal interpretation does Lawrence give to the old story?

The Horses

Edwin Muir

Barely a twelvemonth after
The seven days war that put the world to sleep,
Late in the evening the strange horses came.
By then we had made our covenant with silence,
But in the first few days it was so still   5
We listened to our breathing and were afraid.
On the second day
The radios failed; we turned the knobs; no answer.
On the third day a warship passed us, heading north,
Dead bodies piled on the deck. On the sixth day   10
A plane plunged over us into the sea. Thereafter
Nothing. The radios dumb;
And still they stand in corners of our kitchens,
And stand, perhaps, turned on, in a million rooms
All over the world. But now if they should speak,   15
If on a sudden they should speak again,
If on the stroke of noon a voice should speak,
We would not listen, we would not let it bring
That old bad world that swallowed its children quick
At one great gulp. We would not have it again.   20
Sometimes we think of the nations lying asleep,

Curled blindly in impenetrable sorrow,
And then the thought confounds us with its strange-
    ness.
The tractors lie about our fields; at evening
They look like dank sea-monsters couched and
    waiting.   25
We leave them where they are and let them rust:
'They'll moulder away and be like other loam'.
We make our oxen drag our rusty ploughs,
Long laid aside. We have gone back
Far past our fathers' land.   30
                          And then, that evening
Late in the summer the strange horses came.
We heard a distant tapping on the road,
A deepening drumming; it stopped, went on again
And at the corner changed to hollow thunder.   35
We saw the heads
Like a wild wave charging and were afraid.
We had sold our horses in our fathers' time
To buy new tractors. Now they were strange to us
As fabulous steeds set on an ancient shield   40
Or illustrations in a book of knights.
We did not dare go near them. Yet they waited,
Stubborn and shy, as if they had been sent
By an old command to find our whereabouts
And that long-lost archaic companionship.   45
In the first moment we had never a thought
That they were creatures to be owned and used.
Among them were some half-a-dozen colts
Dropped in some wilderness of the broken world,
Yet new as if they had come from their own Eden.   50
Since then they have pulled our ploughs and borne
    our loads
But that free servitude still can pierce our hearts.
Our life is changed; their coming our beginning.

1. What elements in "The Horses" have been borrowed from myth or folklore? Does the poem serve as a parable for our time? Explain.

2. What makes the horses so important to the poem? Do they act as a symbol of an age past? If so, what age?

3. A certain disturbing quality is established in the very first line of the poem. Can you define it? Does that quality persist throughout the poem? How is it related to contemporary life?

Like the Greek myths, stories from the great religions have been endlessly retold in poems. Their reinterpretation in this century can tell us many things about the times we live in. The following poems, based on the nativity story, are revealingly different from the traditional telling.

Journey of the Magi

T. S. Eliot

'A cold coming we had of it,
Just the worst time of the year
For a journey, and such a long journey:
The ways deep and the weather sharp,
The very dead of winter.'*   5
And the camels galled, sore-footed, refractory,
Lying down in the melting snow.
There were times we regretted

1–5: A cold . . . winter: *adapted by Eliot from a seventeenth-century Christmas sermon.*

The summer palaces on slopes, the terraces,
And the silken girls bringing sherbet.   10
Then the camel men cursing and grumbling
And running away, and wanting their liquor and
      women,
And the night-fires going out, and the lack of shelters,
And the cities hostile and the towns unfriendly
And the villages dirty and charging high prices: 15
A hard time we had of it.
At the end we preferred to travel all night,
Sleeping in snatches,
With the voices singing in our ears, saying
That this was all folly.   20

Then at dawn we came down to a temperate valley,
Wet, below the snow line, smelling of vegetation,
With a running stream and a water-mill beating the
      darkness,
And three trees on the low sky.
And an old white horse galloped away in the meadow.   25
Then we came to a tavern with vine-leaves over the
      lintel,
Six hands at an open door dicing for pieces of silver,
And feet kicking the empty wine-skins.
But there was no information, and so we continued
And arrived at evening, not a moment too soon   30
Finding the place; it was (you may say) satisfactory.

All this was a long time ago, I remember,
And I would do it again, but set down
This set down
This: were we led all that way for   35
Birth or Death? There was a Birth, certainly,
We had evidence and no doubt. I had seen birth and
      death,
But had thought they were different; this Birth was
Hard and bitter agony for us, like Death, our death.

We returned to our places, these Kingdoms,   40
But no longer at ease here, in the old dispensation,
With an alien people clutching their gods.
I should be glad of another death.

The Gift

William Carlos Williams

As the wise men of old brought gifts
        guided by a star
                to the humble birthplace

of the god of love,
        the devils   5
                as an old print shows
retreated in confusion.

        What could a baby know
                of gold ornaments
or frankincense and myrrh,   10
        of priestly robes
                and devout genuflections?

But the imagination
        knows all stories
                before they are told   15
and knows the truth of this one
        past all defection.

The rich gifts
        so unsuitable for a child
                though devoutly proferred,   20
stood for all that love can bring.
        The men were old
                how could they know

of a mother's needs
　　　　or a child's　　　　　　　　　　25
　　　　　　　appetite?

But as they kneeled
　　　　the child was fed.
　　　　　　They saw it
and　　　　　　　　　　　　　　　　30
　　　　gave praise!
　　　　　　A miracle

had taken place,
　　　　hard gold to love,
a mother's milk!　　　　　　　　　　35
　　　　before
　　　　　　their wondering eyes.

The ass brayed
　　　　the cattle lowed.
　　　　　　It was their nature.　　　40

All men by their nature give praise.
　　　　It is all
　　　　　　they can do.

The very devils
　　　　by their flight give praise.　　45
　　　　　　What is death,
beside this?
　　　　Nothing. The wise men
　　　　　　came with gifts

and bowed down　　　　　　　　　50
　　　　to worship
　　　　　　this perfection.

1.　What is surprising and original in the retelling of the old story in
　　each of the last two poems — in point of view? in time element? in
　　selection of detail?

2. The speaker in Eliot's poem is, of course, one of the magi. What has been the impact of this experience for him? Can you see qualities of twentieth-century man in this magus? The special tone and cadence, even the syntax, are revealing. What does the journey mean?

3. A critic wrote that Eliot's "method of exposing the tangle of feeling" was to present it in a series of cinematic images, even when they were subjective. "Impressions, voices, images, dramatic glimpses and poses provide a varied surface." Can you relate some of these elements to "Journey of the Magi" or to "Marina" (page 159)?

4. Compare the tone and images of Eliot's poem with that of Williams's. What reasons can you give for the unusual arrangement of lines in "The Gift"?

Some poems make a game out of the mixing of reality and its double in metaphor. The poet enjoys the game of hide-and-seek, for though his intention is serious, he need not be heavy with the poem.

For One Moment

David Ignatow

You take the dollar
and hand it to the fellow beside you
who turns and gives it to the next one
down the line. The world being round,
you stand waiting, smoking and lifting   5
a cup of coffee to your lips, talking
of seasonal weather and hinting
at problems. The dollar returns,

the coffee spills to the ground
in your hurry. You have the money   10
in one hand, a cup in the other,
a cigarette in your mouth,
and for one moment have forgotten
what it is you have to do,
your hair grey, your legs weakened   15
from long standing.

Things

Louis Simpson

A man stood in the laurel tree
Adjusting his hands and feet to the boughs.
He said, "Today I was breaking stones
On a mountain road in Asia,

When suddenly I had a vision   5
Of mankind, like grass and flowers,
The same over all the earth.
We forgave each other; we gave ourselves
Wholly over to words.
And straightway I was released   10
And sprang through an open gate."

I said, "Into a meadow?"

He said, "I am impervious to irony.
I thank you for the word. . . .
I am standing in a sunlit meadow.   15
Know that everything your senses reject
Springs up in the spiritual world."

I said, "Our scientists have another opinion.
They say, you are merely phenomena."*

He said, "Over here they will be angels   20
Singing, Holy holy be His Name!
And also, it works in reverse.
Things which to us in the pure state are mysterious,
Are your simplest articles of household use —
A chair, a dish, and meaner even than these,   25
The very latest inventions.
Machines are the animals of the Americans —
Tell me about machines."

I said, "I have suspected
The Mixmaster knows more than I do,   30
The air conditioner is the better poet.
My right front tire is as bald as Odysseus —
How much it must have suffered!

Then, as things have a third substance
Which is obscure to both our senses,   35
Let there be a perpetual coming and going
Between your house and mine."

19. phenomena: *here, something known only through the senses.*

I Know a Man

Robert Creeley

As I sd to my
friend, because I am
always talking, — John, I

sd, which was not his
name, the darkness sur-   5
rounds us, what

can we do against
it, or else, shall we &
why not, buy a goddamn big car,

drive, he sd, for   10
christ's sake, look
out where yr going.

1. What point does each of the last three poems make in a paradoxical way? Does each embody a contemporary myth?

2. What undertones of meaning do you find in these poems that are at variance with their playfulness?

3. Which poem interested you most? Which best succeeds, in your opinion, in fusing metaphor with literal reality?

In some poems the literal reality is so complete that the reader may be caught there, unable to see beyond at first. The experience is something like looking at a scene mirrored in a still pool, then, suddenly seeing through the reflection down into a very different and active life inside the water.

Suzanne Takes You Down

Leonard Cohen

Suzanne takes you down
to her place near the river,
you can hear the boats go by
you can stay the night beside her.
And you know that she's half crazy   5
but that's why you want to be there
and she feeds you tea and oranges
that come all the way from China.
Just when you mean to tell her
that you have no gifts to give her,   10
she gets you on her wave-length
and she lets the river answer
that you've always been her lover.
  And you want to travel with her,
  you want to travel blind   15
  and you know that she can trust you
  because you've touched her perfect body
  with your mind.

Jesus was a sailor
when he walked upon the water   20
and he spent a long time watching
from a lonely wooden tower
and when he knew for certain

only drowning men could see him
he said All men will be sailors then   25
until the sea shall free them,
but he himself was broken
long before the sky would open,
forsaken, almost human,
he sank beneath your wisdom like a stone.   30
    And you want to travel with him,
      you want to travel blind
      and you think maybe you'll trust him
      because he touched your perfect body
      with his mind.   35

Suzanne takes your hand
and she leads you to the river,
she is wearing rags and feathers
from Salvation Army counters.
The sun pours down like honey   40
on our lady of the harbour
as she shows you where to look
among the garbage and the flowers,
there are heroes in the seaweed
there are children in the morning,   45
they are leaning out for love
they will lean that way forever
while Suzanne she holds the mirror.
    And you want to travel with her
      and you want to travel blind   50
      and you're sure that she can find you
      because she's touched her perfect body
      with her mind.

June

Bink Noll

"and the name of the chamber
was Peace"

Not time in a rush but whole time
kept waiting outside the windows.
Not a sound but bird. Birdsong
like sun asleep on green surfaces.

Not space packed but opaque shades open   5
to brim light in these bare walls and twin,
the mirror's room. Floor bare as a cell's
with one absolute orange on a sill.

Waking to a whiff of stable
from this brass bed — a risen I   10
as if pencilled on white paper:
the high-ceilinged, palatine,* white light

and my mind like water caught
in a stone basin, its knowledge
privately, in silence, rising   15
now spills over the rim. And spills.

12. palatine: *palace-like.*

When Snow Falls

Katherine Hoskins

It's as though
I had been very happy
Once, maybe was often happy,
And there was snow;

      For years ago,   5
From warmth and strength of nurse or lover leaning
me window-ward, I'd always seen
      The falling snow.

      Now sole specific
For my ill, this flock-meal white has roused   10
That old expectancy; unhoused
      Serene Atlantic

      Bays of being,
Lately forgot; happiness, of late
Forgot. Chaos of face and thing erased,   15
      Abstracts of seeing

      Hold me still.
This mildest magister very air
Of the years' strata has deftly unlayered
      And tranquil   20

My spirit walks
In pathèd sky fields. Royal meander.
Pleasaunce* of saints and nature-worshippers;
      So bred, so taught

    To high estate   25
They're gravelled, like rich heirs, by its lack.
But I'm unused to, poor in fact
      In God or lakes.

    A human gesture
Lacking, on grey unhurried clouds I wait   30
Must patiently, on snow-fall for this late
      Late investiture.

23. Pleasaunce: *feeling or place of pleasure.*

1. Since the rhythms of music are different from those of poetry, it is important to hear "Suzanne" sung. It is also interesting to compare different interpretations of this song — by Leonard Cohen, Judy Collins, and Chad Mitchell, for example. Why do you think this song was so popular?

2. What analogies does the poem make between Suzanne and Christ? Do you recognize other religious motifs? Other ambiguous but powerful images are the river, and the "tea and oranges that come all the way from China." Why was Christ "forsaken" and "almost human"? How does he "[sink] beneath your wisdom like a stone"?

3. How do "June" and "When Snow Falls" help you to understand the quality of peace? Discuss the religious associations in "June." What is the relation of the mirror to the main theme? the orange? the stable? the stone basin? Do you think Katherine Hoskins's poem has religious significance?

4. Many of the unusual terms in "When Snow Falls" have historical associations. What special ambience surrounds such words as "specific," "magister," "pleasaunce," and "investiture"?

The next few poems are highly original in their use of metaphor. In each case the metaphor is extended to include the whole poem. In such poems form is of the highest importance.

Again, in reading these poems, it is useful to approach them in the way suggested on page 16: read first for the shape, then for the sound, and finally for the images. Several readings may be needed to absorb each poem.

Marina

T. S. Eliot

*Quis hic locus, quae
regio, quae mundi plaga?**

What seas what shores what grey rocks and what
    islands
What water lapping the bow
And scent of pine and the woodthrush singing
    through the fog
What images return
O my daughter.   5

Those who sharpen the tooth of the dog, meaning
Death
Those who glitter with the glory of the hummingbird,
    meaning
Death
Those who sit in the sty of contentment, meaning   10
Death

"Marina": *Marina in Shakespeare's* Pericles *was born at sea (hence her name), and lost at sea; her father never expected to see her again, but she was found.*
* Quis hic . . . mundi plaga: *"What place is this, What region, What quarter of the world?" These words were spoken by Hercules in a Roman play, when he awoke from a spell, gradually realizing that he had killed his family.*

Those who suffer the ecstasy of the animals, meaning
Death

Are become unsubstantial, reduced by a wind,
A breath of pine, and the woodsong fog   15
By this grace dissolved in place

What is this face, less clear and clearer
The pulse in the arm, less strong and stronger —
Given or lent? more distant than stars and nearer than
    the eye

Whispers and small laughter between leaves and
    hurrying feet   20
Under sleep, where all the waters meet.

Bowsprit cracked with ice and paint cracked with heat.

I made this, I have forgotten
And remember.
The rigging weak and the canvas rotten   25
Between one June and another September.
Made this unknowing, half conscious, unknown, my
    own.
The garboard strake leaks, the seams need caulking.
This form, this face, this life
Living to live in a world of time beyond me; let me   30
Resign my life for this life, my speech for that un-
    spoken,
The awakened, lips parted, the hope, the new ships.

What seas what shores what granite islands towards
    my timbers
And woodthrush calling through the fog
My daughter.   35

1. As a religious experience of a new life, how expressive are the images of the young daughter, sea, fog, and birdsong? What does the boat seem to mean in terms of journey? It is important to follow the images in sequence, since they precisely define the journey.

2. Notice the heavy incantatory beat of the second stanza with its ugly symbols and sounds. What effect has this stanza on the strong lyrical quality of the poem? What does this stanza mean?

3. Compare the style of "Marina" with that of "Journey of the Magi" (page 145) and with "The Hollow Men" (page 9).

The Arrival of the Bee Box

Sylvia Plath

I ordered this, this clean wood box
Square as a chair and almost too heavy to lift.
I would say it was the coffin of a midget
Or a square baby
Were there not such a din in it.   5

The box is locked, it is dangerous.
I have to live with it overnight
And I can't keep away from it.
There are no windows, so I can't see what is in there.
There is only a little grid, no exit.   10

I put my eye to the grid.
It is dark, dark,
With the swarmy feeling of African hands
Minute and shrunk for export,
Black on black, angrily clambering.   15

How can I let them out?
It is the noise that appals me most of all,

The unintelligible syllables.
It is like a Roman mob,
Small, taken one by one, but my god, together!   20

I lay my ear to furious Latin.
I am not a Caesar.
I have simply ordered a box of maniacs.
They can be sent back.
They can die, I need feed them nothing, I am the
        owner.   25

I wonder how hungry they are.
I wonder if they would forget me
If I just undid the locks and stood back and turned
        into a tree.
There is the laburnum, its blond colonnades,
And the petticoats of the cherry.   30

They might ignore me immediately
In my moon suit and funeral veil.
I am no source of honey
So why should they turn on me?
Tomorrow I will be sweet God, I will set them free.   35

The box is only temporary.

1. Discuss the development of sound and feeling in this poem that
    starts with the monstrous images of the first stanza, at last shifts in
    the sixth to the "blond colonnades" of the laburnum, and then to
    "moon suit and funeral veil." What is the dominant mood? What
    do you think the bee box represents?

2. Some critics have thought that the bees are a symbol for the cre-
    ative impulses that lead to the writing of poetry. What, then, seems
    to have been Sylvia Plath's conception of the poet's obligations?

The Waking

Theodore Roethke

I wake to sleep, and take my waking slow.
I feel my fate in what I cannot fear.
I learn by going where I have to go.

We think by feeling. What is there to know?
I hear my being dance from ear to ear.   5
I wake to sleep, and take my waking slow.

Of those so close beside me, which are you?
God bless the Ground! I shall walk softly there,
And learn by going where I have to go.

Light takes the Tree; but who can tell us how?   10
The lowly worm climbs up a winding stair;
I wake to sleep, and take my waking slow.

Great Nature has another thing to do
To you and me; so take the lively air,
And, lovely, learn by going where to go.   15

This shaking keeps me steady. I should know.
What falls away is always. And is near.
I wake to sleep, and take my waking slow.
I learn by going where I have to go.

1. How does the reiteration of the key lines, each seemingly vague in itself, nevertheless lead to an understanding of this poem? The few, and therefore important, images are also revealing, as is the use of capitals. What kind of waking is this? What kind of going? of knowing?

2. The villanelle is an intricate and seldom used form. Why do you think Roethke found it useful for this poem? It is interesting to compare the very different way in which Dylan Thomas used the form in "Do Not Go Gentle into That Good Night" (page 100).

Lemuel's Blessing

W. S. Merwin

> *Let Lemuel bless with the wolf, which is a
> dog without a master, but the Lord hears
> his cries and feeds him in the desert.*
> CHRISTOPHER SMART: *Jubilate Agno**

You that know the way,
Spirit,
I bless your ears which are like cypruses on a mountain
With their roots in wisdom. Let me approach.
I bless your paws and their twenty nails which tell
    their own prayer   5
And are like dice in command of their own com-
    binations.
Let me not be lost.
I bless your eyes for which I know no comparison.
Run with me like the horizon, for without you
I am nothing but a dog lost and hungry,   10
Ill-natured, untrustworthy, useless.

My bones together bless you like an orchestra of flutes.
Divert the weapons of the settlements and lead their
    dogs a dance.
Where a dog is shameless and wears servility
In his tail like a banner,   15
Let me wear the opprobrium of possessed and
    possessors
As a thick tail properly used
To warm my worst and my best parts. My tail and my
    laugh bless you.

---

* *Lemuel, in the Bible (Proverbs 31:1–31), was a good and just king. Christo-
pher Smart, an eighteenth-century English poet and journalist, wrote the in-
coherent poem* Jubilate Agno *("Rejoice in the Lamb") while confined to an
asylum.*

Lead me past the error at the fork of hesitation.
Deliver me   20

From the ruth of the lair, which clings to me in the
    morning,
Painful when I move, like a trap;
Even debris has its favorite positions but they are not
    yours;
From the ruth of kindness, with its licked hands;
I have sniffed baited fingers and followed   25
Toward necessities which were not my own: it would
    make me
An habitué of back steps, faithful custodian of fat
    sheep;

From the ruth of prepared comforts, with its
Habitual dishes sporting my name and its collars and
    leashes of vanity;

From the ruth of approval, with its nets, kennels, and
    taxidermists;   30
It would use my guts for its own rackets and instru-
    ments, to play its own games and music;
Teach me to recognize its platforms, which are con-
    structed like scaffolds;

From the ruth of known paths, which would use my
    feet, tail, and ears as curios,
My head as a nest for tame ants,
My fate as a warning.   35

I have hidden at wrong times for wrong reasons.
I have been brought to bay. More than once.
Another time, if I need it,
Create a little wind like a cold finger between my
    shoulders, then
Let my nails pour out a torrent of aces like grain from
    a threshing machine;   40

Let fatigue, weather, habitation, the old bones, finally,
Be nothing to me,
Let all lights but yours be nothing to me.
Let the memory of tongues not unnerve me so that I
    stumble or quake.
But lead me at times beside the still waters;   45
There when I crouch to drink let me catch a glimpse
    of your image
Before it is obscured with my own.

Preserve my eyes, which are irreplaceable.
Preserve my heart, veins, bones,
Against the slow death building in them like hornets
    until the place is entirely theirs.   50
Preserve my tongue and I will bless you again and
    again.

Let my ignorance and my failings
Remain far behind me like tracks made in a wet
    season,
At the end of which I have vanished,
So that those who track me for their own twisted ends   55
May be rewarded only with ignorance and failings.
But let me leave my cry stretched out behind me like
    a road
On which I have followed you.
And sustain me for my time in the desert
On what is essential to me.   60

1. The theme of this enigmatic poem seems more mysterious on the
   literal level than on the metaphorical. Consider it, then, literally:
   Whose voice do we hear speaking? What do you discover by its
   tone? Be aware of the biblical echoes in the parallelisms and
   sweeping rhythms. If this is a prayer, what is he praying for? To
   whom — a wolf spirit? (American Indians and other tribal people,
   closer to the natural world than we, used to be chosen by the

spirit of a certain animal and were proud to take his character and name. Has this any bearing on the poem as you read it?)

2. Can you relate this poem to the present day? — a poem is completely of its own time, and can only use other material to express its own meanings.

The movement toward the irrational in twentieth-century poetry has gone much further in French and Spanish than it has in the poetry of the English-speaking world. The Spanish poet García Lorca, for instance, has been an influence on many English-speaking poets, but few have been able to open the doors to the subconscious so freely.

Lorca's "Somnambulistic Ballad" is reminiscent of surrealism,* except that the images are always moving, forming and reforming, instead of remaining static. The special strengths of this kind of free association are reflected in LeRoi Jones's poem, which follows Lorca's.

Somnambulistic Ballad

Federico García Lorca

translated by Roy and Mary Campbell

Green, green, I want you green
Green the wind and green the boughs.
The ship upon the ocean seen.
The horses on the hills that browse.

---

* surrealism: *a movement in twentieth-century writing which attempts to synthesize the experiences of the conscious and unconscious mind by drawing on the materials of dream and automatic association.*

With the shadows round her waist   5
Upon her balcony she dreams.
Green her flesh and green her tresses.
In her eyes chill silver gleams.
Green, green, I want you green
While the gypsy moon beam plays,   10
Things at her are gazing keenly
But she cannot meet their gaze.

Green, green, I want you green.
See the great stars of the frost
Come rustling with the fish of shadow   15
To find the way the dawn has lost.
The figtree chafes the passing wind
With the sandpaper of its leaves,
And hissing like a thievish cat,
With bristled fur, the mountain heaves.   20
But who will come? And by what path?
On her verandah lingers she,
Green her flesh and green her hair,
Dreaming of the bitter sea.

     'Companion, I should like to trade   25
My pony for your house and grange,
To swap my saddle for your mirror,
My sheath-knife for your rug to change.
Companion, I have galloped bleeding
From Cabra's passes down the range,'   30
     'If it could be arranged, my lad,
I'd clinch the bargain; but you see
Now I am no longer I,
Nor does my house belong to me.'
     'Companion, I should like to die   35
Respectably at home in bed,
A bed of steel if possible,
With sheets of linen smoothly spread.
Can you not see this gash I carry
From rib to throat, from chin to chest?' 40

'Three hundred roses darkly red
Spatter the white front of your vest.
Your blood comes oozing out to spread,
Around your sash, its ghostly smell.
But now I am no longer I   45
Nor is my house my own to sell.'

Let me go up tonight at least,
And climb the dim verandah's height.
Let me go up! Oh let me climb
To the verandah green with light,   50
Oh chill verandahs of the moon
Whence fall the waters of the night!

And now the two companions climb
Up where the high verandah sheers,
Leaving a little track of blood,   55
Leaving a little trail of tears.
Trembling along the roofs, a thousand
Sparkles of tin reflect the ray.
A thousand tambourines of glass
Wounded the dawning of the day.   60

Green, green, I want you green.
Green the wind: and green the bough.
The two companions clambered up
And a long wind began to sough
Which left upon the mouth a savour   65
Of gall and mint and basil-flowers.
Companion! Tell me. Where is she?
Where is that better girl of ours?
How many times she waited for you!
How long she waited, hoped, and sighed,   70
Fresh her face, and black her tresses,
Upon this green verandah-side!

Over the surface of the pond
The body of the gypsy sways.
Green her flesh and green her tresses   75
Her eyes a frosty silver glaze.
An icicle hung from the moon —
Suspends her from the water there.
The night became as intimate
As if it were the village square.   80
The drunkards of the Civil Guard,
Banging the door, began to swear.
Green, oh green, I want you green.
Green the wind: and green the boughs
The ship upon the water seen   85
The horses on the hill that browse.

Lines to García Lorca

LeRoi Jones

Climin up the mountin, chillun,
Didn't come here for to stay,
If I'm ever gonna see you agin,
It'll be on the judgment day.

NEGRO SPIRITUAL

Send soldiers again to kill you, García.
Send them to quell my escape.
These things mean nothing.
You are dying again, García.
This is all I remember.   5
Send soldiers again, García.
Hail Mary,
Holy mother,
Pray for me.

I live near a mountain, green mirror   10
Of burning paths and a low sun

To measure my growing by.
There is a wind that repeats
A bird's name and near his
Cage is a poem, and a small boy herding   15
Cattle with diamonds
In their mouths.

Mandolins grow on the high slopes
And orange-robed monks collect songs
Just beyond the last line of fruit trees.   20
Naked girls pretend they are butterflies,
And a deer tells stories to the twilight.

García, where is my Bible?
I want to read those myths
Again.   No answer,   25
But, away off, quite close to the daylight,
I hear his voice, and he is laughing, laughing
Like a Spanish guitar.

Because it has dispensed with all explanations and transitions, the following poem by W. S. Merwin may at first appear to belong to the surrealist, or European, tradition. Actually, however, the poem is grounded in a more rational, and literal, reality.

The Removal

To the Endless Tribe

W. S. Merwin

1
The Procession

When we see
the houses again
we will know that we are asleep at last

when we see
tears on the road
and they are ourselves   5
we are awake
the tree has been cut
on which we were leaves
the day does not know us   10
the river where we cross does not taste salt

the soles of our feet are black stars
but ours is the theme
of the light

2
The Homeless

A clock keeps striking   15
and the echoes move in files
their faces
have been lost
flowers of salt
tongues from lost languages   20
doorways closed with pieces of night

3
A Survivor

The dust never settles
but through it tongue tongue comes walking
shuffling like breath
but the old speech
is still in its country   25
dead

4
The Crossing of the Removed

At the bottom of the river
black ribbons cross under
and the water tries to soothe them   30
the mud tries to soothe them
the stones turn over and over trying
to comfort them
but they will not be healed

where the rims cut   35
and the shadows
sawed carrying
mourners
and some that had used horses
and had the harness   40
dropped it in half way over
on the far side the ribbons come out
invisible

5
A Widow is Taken

I call leave me here
the smoke on the black path   45
was my children
I will not walk
from the house I warmed
but they carry me through the light
my blackening face   50
my red eyes
everywhere I leave
one white footprint

the trackers will follow us into the cold
the water is high   55
the boats have been stolen away
there are no shoes
and they pretend that I am a bride
on the way to a new house

6
The Reflection

Passing a broken window   60
they see
into each of them the wedge of blackness
pounded
it is nothing
it splits them   65
loose hair
bare heels
at last they are gone
filing on in vacant rooms

INDEX OF TITLES AND AUTHORS

ILLUSTRATION CREDITS